Western Frontiersmen Series
XII

WILLIAM WOLFSKILL
From an oil painting at Zion National Park.

WILLIAM WOLFSKILL

1798-1866

Frontier Trapper to
California Ranchero

by

Iris Higbie Wilson

The Arthur H. Clark Company
Glendale, California
1965

to

MY MOTHER AND FATHER

Mr. and Mrs. Clarence Alden Higbie

Contents

Illustrations

Preface

A pioneer, by definition, is a person who goes before – one who prepares the way for others. America is rich in pioneering lore, but not even Horatio Alger would have dared create a character who prepared the way in as many fields as William Wolfskill. As a fur trapper and Santa Fe trader, Wolfskill explored uncharted areas of the Southwest – and then blazed a new trail to California. As one of the first American settlers to remain in Mexico's Pacific coast province as a permanent resident, Wolfskill pioneered in numerous agricultural and related economic activities. Known to many persons simply as "the Kentucky trapper," Wolfskill founded California's citrus industry, joined in the establishment of its wine industry, sponsored the state's first public school in Los Angeles, and aided in the development of southern California's cattle industry. Further, Wolfskill was always ready to give assistance to his fellow citizens and to support the community in which he lived.

Because the native *Californios* considered all people born east of the Rocky Mountains as "Yanquis," Wolfskill's story becomes part of the tradition of Yankee ingenuity at work on the frontier. From the time of his arrival in 1831 until his death in 1866, Don Guillermo, as he was affectionately called by his Hispanic neighbors, exerted an active, although quiet, influence on the economic, political and cultural life of California. His thirty-five year residency as a *yanqui ranchero* allowed Wolfskill to play an important role in California's transformation from a sleepy Mexican province to a state in which America's manifest destiny was fulfilled.

My interest in Wolfskill's life was first aroused through lectures on the history of California given by Professor Donald C. Cutter at the University of Southern California. With Dr. Cutter's encouragement and direction, I decided to undertake further investigation. Subsequent research proved that Wolfskill had received mention in almost every history of California covering the period from 1830 to 1866, and was included in many specialized works on the fur trade, California agriculture, and Los Angeles history. In spite of his obvious importance, a volume covering all of Wolfskill's activities has been nonexistent. It is my purpose to illustrate the significance of William Wolfskill not only as a "Kentucky trapper," mountain man and pathfinder, but as a pioneer agriculturist and leading citizen of southern California.

I wish to express my gratitude for the many courtesies extended to me by the staff members of the Bancroft Library at the University of California, Berkeley; the Henry E. Huntington Library, San Marino, California; the City Archives of Los Angeles; the State Archives of New Mexico, Santa Fe; and the other depositories of source material pertinent to this study.

Special thanks are given to Miss Linda L. McKinney and Mr. Luis A. Gallego in sincere appreciation of their stenographic and research assistance; and to Mrs. Thomas Paul Cullen for her kindness in allowing me to use the diaries of her grandfather, Henry Dwight Barrows.

My investigation for the present work was made infinitely more enjoyable through the encouragement of William Wolfskill's grandson, Mr. John Christian Wolfskill of Los Angeles. I am particularly indebted to him, to his wife Lucretia Phelps Wolfskill, and to other descendants of the Wolfskill family for their indispensable cooperation in providing information concerning the life of their pioneer ancestor.

William Wolfskill

Pioneer Origins

O you youths, Western youths,
So impatient, full of action,
                    full of manly pride and friendship
Plain I see you, Western youths,
                    see you tramping with the foremost
Pioneers! O pioneers!

– Walt Whitman

William Wolfskill was born in Boonesborough, Kentucky, on March 20, 1798, but his story does not begin on that day. It begins with the settling of America by northern Europeans in the mid-eighteenth century, alters its course slightly with the winning of American independence, and receives an additional thrust with the opening of new lands beyond the Appalachian mountains. The same conditions responsible for creating the first generation of American pioneers would in turn influence the ambitions and desires of the Wolfskills and other families moving westward in search of new opportunities after the American Revolution. For them, the frontier offered a better life.

There is no definite answer to the question of what makes a pioneer, but one can find part of the evidence by going back to the Kentucky wilderness – to the land which fostered the pioneering spirits of Daniel Boone, Kit Carson, Sylvester and James Ohio Pattie,

the Sublette brothers, and a host of others. Daniel
Boone first settled in Madison County, Kentucky,
the birthplace of William Wolfskill, in the year
1775. Just as Daniel Boone successfully overcame the
hardships of blazing a new trail westward, William
Wolfskill would, a generation later, extend this great
path to the very edge of the American continent – to
California.

The opening of the Wilderness Road by Daniel
Boone's party in the mid-1770's was an event which
played a significant role in the phase of American
pioneering life which began in that decade. The men
who left North Carolina in March of 1775 under
Boone's leadership first traveled across Powell's
Valley, in what is now the northwestern corner of
that state, and then made their way through the
Cumberland Gap. They blazed and cleared a trail
for fifty miles until a well-worn buffalo trace luckily
provided a pathway leading toward the West. After
cutting their way through thick brush for twenty
miles along the Rockcastle River, these pioneers were
able to follow another buffalo trace for an additional
thirty miles. The last lap brought the men to that
portion of the Kentucky River located in present-day
Madison County. Daniel Boone chose a valley lined
with sycamores as the site on which to build Boonesborough. One member of the party wrote: "Perhaps
no Adventureor Since the days of donquicksotte [Don
Quixote] or before ever felt So Cheerful & Ilated
. . . to discover the pleasing & Rapturous appear-

ance of the plains of Kentucky, a New Sky & Strange Earth." [1]

Madison County was not, however, to remain quite so "pleasing and rapturous" as had first been imagined. After several Indian attacks, complete with scalpings, some of the weaker spirits in Boone's party hurriedly returned to North Carolina. But those with courage and determination stayed on, for neither wilderness hardships nor Indians could conquer their will. Men began clearing the land and building shelters to make way for other parties of settlers who were not far behind. Included among a half dozen families from Virginia was a certain Abraham Hanks, uncle of Nancy Hanks, mother of Abraham Lincoln. After once turning back because of reports of Indian attacks, Hanks met another group headed for Kentucky, changed his mind, and reached Madison County after all. Such were the pre-revolutionary treks into the wilderness; journeys which would bring families to the little town of Boonesborough and eventually to other great areas of the "West." [2]

Back in North Carolina a neighbor of Daniel Boone was considering the prospect of taking his wife and family into this new and fertile territory of Kentucky. The man was a husky, pioneering German farmer from the Pennsylvania country, and was

---

[1] John Bakeless, *Daniel Boone* (New York, 1939), 90.

[2] *Ibid.*, 91; G. C. Broadhead, "Daniel Boone," in *Missouri Historical Review*, III (January 1909), 89-98.

known by the name of Joseph Wolfskill.[3] As the youngest of seven brothers who, because of their height and physical fitness, had been impressed into the service of Frederick the Great as members of his famous Potsdam regiment, Joseph Wolfskill fled to America in 1742 to escape similar duty in the king's guard. This story, which had been passed down through the Wolfskill family, was substantiated when a Doctor William Wolfskehl of Germany arrived in San Francisco, via Australia, on his return home to Germany in 1870, and later when his son came from Berlin to inspect the Northern Pacific Railroad. Dr. Wolfskehl stated that his grandfather was one of seven brothers of whom Frederick the Great had impressed six into his Potsdam regiment of tall men and that his grandfather was the only one of the six that escaped from the wars, leaving the Wolfskehls of Germany as his descendants. Dr. Wolfskehl said further that the seventh and youngest brother had come to America, and both the doctor and his son believed that the Wolfskills of Kentucky and later California were descendants of this younger brother.[4]

Joseph and his wife, Margaret Smith Wolfskill, like their neighbor Daniel Boone, had been schooled in the hard and rugged life of the pioneer in the frontier regions of Pennsylvania. Now the same enticements which had brought a steady movement of

---

[3] U.S. Census 179 of Franklin County, Pennsylvania, in *Pennsylvania Archives,* 5th Series, VI, p. 119.

[4] James M. Guinn, *A History of California and an Extended History of Los Angeles and Environs* (Los Angeles, 1915), II, p. 24.

settlers from Pennsylvania to the rich lands of the Shenandoah Valley and to the fertile regions of North Carolina were beckoning Joseph Wolfskill to push westward with his family to the vast lands beyond the Appalachians.[5]

During the same period, a different set of circumstances were working to bring another important individual to Madison County, Kentucky. John Reid had come to America from Ireland and served as a soldier in the Revolutionary War. He was captured by the British at Charleston, South Carolina, and forced to remain there until the end of the war. Following his release, John Reid set out to find his cousin, Nathan Reid, whom he learned was associated with Daniel Boone, Richard Callaway and Richard Henderson in some Kentucky land speculation. By the end of the war the problem of Indian attacks had been almost completely overcome and Boonesborough, Madison County, was experiencing the transformation into a well-established settlement. At cousin Nathan's encouragement, John Reid decided to join this frontier community and so brought to Kentucky his wife and family and no small amount of Scotch-Irish determination.[6]

In the spring of 1797 young Joseph Wolfskill, Jr. began seriously courting the daughter of his father's friend and neighbor John Reid. The romance between Joseph and Sarah was the bringing together of

---

[5] The children of Joseph and Margaret Smith Wolfskill were Margaret, George, Peter, William and Joseph, Jr.

[6] Nellie Van de Grift Sanchez, *California and Californians* (Chicago, 1926), III, p. 117.

two hardy pioneer families who had not only braved
the hardship of moving west, but who would encour-
age the young couple to move still further into the
unsettled frontier regions. The marriage of Joseph
Wolfskill, Jr. and Sarah Reid on June 20 was un-
doubtedly solemnized by a typical frontier wedding.[7]
This was an occasion for great celebration, as the
rugged daily life provided little time for relaxation
and a wedding was one of the acceptable excuses for
gathering together the members of the community.
After the exchange of vows, the entire wedding party
usually remained in the cabin where the bride and
groom were to spend their wedding night and partook
of a feast which included the best of backwoods
gourmet cooking. A jug of corn whiskey would be
passed among the men and if the number of toasts
could be used as an index, the young couple was
assured of a long and happy life blessed with many
fine children.

Such were the conditions under which Kentucky
newly-weds like Joseph and Sarah Wolfskill began
their life together. In less than a year a baby son was
born who was destined to carve a significant place for
himself in the new and ever-expanding country of
the United States. Brought into the world on land
which had been opened by one of the great pioneers
of all time, this child would continue to grow in the
tradition of the original pathfinder of the Old West.

---

[7] Annie Walker Burns, "Kentucky Vital Statistics: Records of Marriages
in Madison County, Kentucky, for the period of years 1788 to 1851, inclusive," MS 124, Los Angeles Public Library.

Joseph Wolfskill, Jr. named the child William,[8] and a new generation was launched. During the next ten years in Madison County while little "Billy" Wolfskill was growing up, Joseph and Sarah proceeded to have seven more children – Mathus, Margaret, Stephen, Elizabeth, Suzanna, Joshua and John Reid. Later in Missouri they would complete their already sizable family with Sarchel, Mary, Milton and Smith.

After 1800 Kentucky was no longer on the extreme fringe of settlement. The Indian danger had nearly passed and Madison County had become a peaceful farming region. Among the neighbors of the Wolfskills and the Reids were several prominent pioneer families. Probably the best-known was that sired by William Carson of Scotch-Irish ancestry who had emigrated from Scotland or the north of Ireland to Pennsylvania in the first half of the eighteenth century. Then, following the pattern which transferred much Scotch-Irish protestant blood into Tennessee and the Carolinas, William Carson moved to North Carolina and settled in Iredell County. One of his five sons, Lindsey, journeyed with his wife and family to Madison County in 1794. Mrs. Carson did not long survive the birth of her fourth child, dying soon after her arrival in Madison County. Lindsey married Rebecca Robinson of Virginia in 1797 and she added ten more children to the Carson family. Of

---

[8] It is possible that his first name was Joseph, although he never used it. Upon becoming a Mexican citizen, he took the name of José Guillermo Wolfskill.

these her fifth, a son by the name of Christopher, was destined to become the most famous. Kit Carson was born on December 24, 1809, and like John Reid Wolfskill, was the last of his family to be born before their long trek to Missouri.[9]

As did the Wolfskills and the Carsons, the Cooper family contributed its share to the population of Madison County. In an original account written in 1888, Major Stephen Cooper states that his father, Sarshell Cooper, a captain in the Revolutionary Army, emigrated from Virginia to Kentucky shortly after the war. Both Sarshell and his brother, Lt. Col. Benjamin Cooper, brought their families to Boonesborough to settle, although it was the latter who would lead the rest into the vast, uninhabited forests of the recently acquired Louisiana Territory.[10]

Because the trail through the Cumberland Gap was becoming a regular thoroughfare and settlers were arriving in Madison County in increasing numbers, Benjamin Cooper decided it was time to move on – time to recapture the pleasant solitude of the unsettled regions of the west. In 1808 Colonel Cooper took his wife and five sons to the area of Boone's Lick in what is now Howard County, Missouri, and proceeded to establish a settlement on the fertile soil of the Missouri River bottoms. There he built a cabin, cleared a piece of ground and commenced arrangements for bringing other settlers to this land.

9 Edwin L. Sabin, *Kit Carson Days, 1809-1868* (New York, 1935), 1-4.
10 Stephen Cooper, *Sketches from the Life of Major Stephen Cooper* (Oakland, 1888), 3.

But Benjamin Cooper was not permitted to remain long, because Meriwether Lewis (of Lewis and Clark fame and then governor of the Louisiana territory) ordered him to return to below the mouth of the Gasconade River. Governor Lewis insisted that because Cooper had penetrated so far into Indian country, no protection could be guaranteed for his settlers.

Under these circumstances, the Cooper family was forced to return to Loutre Island below the mouth of the Gasconade, where they remained for two years. They were then joined on the island by twenty-five families, including the Wolfskills, who had set out from Madison County late in 1809. In the spring of 1810, Benjamin Cooper decided to return to his former settlement at Boone's Lick, but this time with his Kentucky neighbors and relatives to clear the land and begin the construction of cabins. Thus were laid the foundations for Boone's Lick Township in what would become Howard County, Missouri. However, this remote area would, like the frontiers of North Carolina and Kentucky, soon become engulfed in the unending wave of settlers extending further and further into the West.[11]

The naming of the township is of historical interest because of its connection with Daniel Boone. It seems that the great pathfinder had built a cabin and camped one winter in the vicinity of the numerous salt springs or "licks" of this area because it was an

---

[11] *History of Howard and Cooper Counties, Missouri* (St. Louis, 1883), 92ff.

ideal place to encounter wild game. The exact date
of his so doing is not known, although it was probably in 1802 or 1803. It is unlikely that Boone himself, a successful hunter and trapper, ever mined salt
there, but his sons, Nathan and Daniel, later proc-
essed salt in the area of Boone's Lick. About 1807
they were conveying their product to the river in
hollow logs and eventually did a business large
enough to supply salt to distant New Orleans.[12]

The settlers who arrived with Benjamin Cooper
had to contend with many difficulties, chief among
which was the opposition of Congress to their occupying lands within the limits set apart for the Indians.
The settlers nevertheless determined not to surrender
their claims, which were derived from a Spanish
grant of the land to Ira P. Nash in the year 1800,
and continued to occupy the territory. The Wolfskills
and their neighbors cleared and fenced a small tract
of land in common and began the business of setting
up a community.[13] A more immediate problem was
that of securing an adequate supply of food. When
the settlers first arrived in the county, wild game was
extremely abundant and furnished the families with
the major item of their diet. It was practically impossible for them to raise any type of crop because
small animals such as squirrels and rabbits swarmed
around their homes in such numbers that constant

[12] Will S. Bryan, "Peculiarities of Life in Daniel Boone's Missouri Settlement," in *Missouri Historical Review*, IV (January 1910), 9; Bakeless,
Daniel Boone, 392.

[13] *History of Howard and Cooper Counties, Missouri*, 92.

killing was necessary in order to save the young
plants. To meet other necessities, the Wolfskills and
their fellow colonists manufactured their own gunpowder, mined their own salt, and supplied themselves with a fabric made from wild nettles which
resembled a cotton material. They managed to raise
some corn from which bread was made, but in general a diet of wild game was easier to maintain.[14]

During the next two years, 1811 and 1812, a large
number of emigrants joined the line of march to the
Boone's Lick country. While St. Louis was still a
small French village serving as headquarters for an
upper-country fur trade, homesteaders were passing
through on their way to the fertile lands along side
the Missouri River. In the spring of 1811 the Missouri Fur Company of St. Louis was being reorganized, and the American Fur Company, spurred
on by its zealous founder, German immigrant John
Jacob Astor, was advancing to the Pacific Coast.
Astor's trading and supply ship "Tonquin" was en
route to the mouth of the Columbia River and its
supporting overland party led by Wilson Price Hunt
had started out from St. Louis along the Missouri
River trail. Also in the spring of 1811 Lindsey Carson moved his wife and family by ox team and wagon
to Boone's Lick.

After the pioneer settlers of Howard County,
Missouri, learned how to protect their crops, conditions in the territory improved considerably. But

[14] Henry D. Barrows, "Story of an Old Pioneer, William Wolfskill," in
Los Angeles *World,* Sept. 24, 1887.

there was still the ever-present danger of Indian attacks which continued to be a serious threat until after the War of 1812. One frontiersman remarked that in the territory there was "no man owing a dollar, no taxes to pay" and that they "lived happy and prosperous until the War of 1812, when the Indians began their depredations." [15] By this time the number of settlers in the area had increased to nearly 21,000, so Congress, on June 4, 1812, set up a separate Missouri Territory and appointed William Clark (also of Lewis and Clark fame) as "Governor and Superintendent of Indian Affairs." [16] This act, however, did little to solve the Indian problem because Governor Clark, with his seat of administration at St. Louis, was either unwilling or unable to guarantee any protection to the settlers at Boone's Lick. Finally, the Wolfskills and their neighbors decided to take matters into their own hands.

Joseph Wolfskill, Benjamin Cooper, Lindsey Carson and a number of others were fully convinced that the Indians were making preparations to attack the settlements along the Missouri River. They believed that their best means of defense lay in the construction of three forts. Fort Cooper was built about two miles southwest of Boone's Lick; Fort Kincaid was built nine miles to the southeast near present-day Boonville; and Fort Hempstead was completed on a site about a mile and one half north of Fort Kincaid.

[15] Barrows, "Story of an Old Pioneer," in Los Angeles *World*, Oct. 1, 1887.

[16] LeRoy R. Hafen and Carl C. Rister, *Western America* (New York, 1954), 205.

Each fort consisted of a series of one family log houses built together around a central enclosure. At night the livestock was corraled and the property of the settlers secured inside the enclosure.[17]

The members of the Wolfskill family were confined in Fort Cooper and forced to remain there until the end of the war in 1815. Evidently the families got along very well together as Stephen Cooper later wrote, "For several years we had no organized government; each did what he thought was right in his own eyes, and we had very little trouble in our own fort – in fact we never had any." [18] As soon as the construction of the forts was completed, the pioneers organized themselves into a military company with Sarshell Cooper as captain; William McMahan, first lieutenant; John Monroe, second lieutenant; and Benjamin Cooper, Jr., ensign. In addition to these officers, there were chosen five sergeants and six corporals to command a company of 112 men capable of bearing arms. At Fort Cooper, Joseph Wolfskill, his older brother William, and a nephew served the company along with several Coopers, Hancocks, Ashcrafts, Jacksons, Greggs, Andersons, Alexanders and Joneses. There were also such individuals as Ezekiel Williams, Gray Bynum, Robert Heath and Robert Irvine serving at Fort Cooper. The Carson family took up duty at nearby Fort Hempstead.[19]

---

[17] *History of Howard and Cooper Counties,* 95.

[18] Cooper, *op. cit.,* 4.

[19] Will C. Ferril, "Missouri Military in the War of 1812," in *Missouri Historical Review,* IV (October 1909), 38-41; *History of Howard and Cooper Counties,* 96.

Even though they were unable to participate in many of their normal activities, the settlers maintained a school for their children and conducted regular religious services within the fort. During the winter season the planters would employ some traveling schoolmaster, who usually applied to himself the distinguished title of "professor," and would insist that the youth of the community learn a few fundamentals at least.[20] The confinement within the fort, however, was somewhat irksome to the younger children and John Reid Wolfskill, then eight years old, long afterwards spoke of it with bitterness. Once while school was in session an alarm of "Indians" was given and he remembered that the older boys immediately dropped their books and grabbed their guns. While the students awaited in fright for an attack, they fortunately received the news that the alarm had resulted from the passing of a large party of Indians on their way to St. Louis to make a treaty with the United States government. This particular incident happened to occur near the end of the war, but up until that time few alarms had turned out to be false.[21]

Throughout the War of 1812 the men of the settlement had to be continually on their guard and carry a gun even while plowing. Ironically, one very sad incident occurred just after the news that peace had been declared reached the fort in 1815. Sarshell

20 Bryan, *op. cit.*, 87.
21 Thomas J. Gregory, *History of Solano and Napa Counties, California* (Los Angeles, 1912), 423.

Cooper was shot and killed instantly by an Indian who had picked a hole in the wall of the fort.[22] The remaining members of the Cooper family, however, as well as all of the Wolfskills, emerged from the war unharmed and not without considerable knowledge gained from the experience.

By the time he had reached the age of fourteen, William Wolfskill had learned to handle a long Kentucky rifle with amazing facility.[23] This aspect of his education was an important supplement to his thorough training in the skills of plowing, planting and the raising of livestock which he had received along with his intermittent instruction in reading and writing, and was essential for self-preservation on the frontier. As a young boy he was also schooled in methods of hunting and trapping, skills which would become basic to his very existence in the uncharted regions to the west. Actually, the training which William Wolfskill received in the Missouri wilderness was the result of two generations of frontier experience. It would serve him well.

After the war, in 1815, William and two of his sisters were sent back to Kentucky to attend school. Upon completion of two years of "formal education," William, now a young man, returned to Missouri and remained at home in Boone's Lick until 1822.[24]

---

[22] Cooper, op. cit., 4.

[23] The Kentucky Rifle, developed by gunsmiths around Lancaster, Pennsylvania, in the 1740's, measured from forty-eight to sixty-two inches and weighed between eight and twelve pounds. The spiral (rifled) bore gave it greater accuracy than a smoothbore musket.

[24] Barrows, in Los Angeles World, Oct. 1, 1887.

With the return of peace, Howard County had been organized under an act of the Territorial Legislature in January of 1816 and was enjoying a new wave of immigration.[25] St. Louis had become a booming trade center, the home of the principal fur companies and the outfitting base for westbound expeditions. At the age of twenty-three "Billy" Wolfskill decided that it was time for him to set out on his own – time to seek his fortune in the rapidly expanding fur trade of the great Southwest – time to carry his family's pioneer tradition into the yet unexplored areas of the Rocky Mountains, the Great Basin, and even those of distant California.

[25] "Some Historic Lines in Missouri," in *Missouri Historical Review,* III (July 1909), 253.

2

On to Santa Fe!

All the past we leave behind,
We debouch upon a newer, mightier world, varied world,
Fresh and strong the world we seize,
> *world of labor and the march*
Pioneers! O pioneers!
> – Walt Whitman

Certainly William Wolfskill had been schooled in a well-rounded curriculum of frontier skills; but it was now time for the young trapper to receive the next phase of his education – that of blazing new trails into the unknown regions of the far Southwest.

Captain William Becknell of Franklin, Missouri, had advertised in the *Missouri Intelligencer* of June 10, 1821, for "seventy men to go westward" on a trading project.[1] Becknell assembled his company at the home of Wolfskill's neighbor, Ezekiel Williams, and plans were made for a journey to Santa Fe, the Spanish capital of New Mexico which had recently become a part of the independent Mexican republic. Becknell's venture was so successful and profitable that when he returned to Missouri in January of 1822, two expeditions were organized to return to

---

[1] Quoted in Sabin, *Kit Carson Days*, 10. Numerous reports of Becknell's and other expeditions of the 1820's are found in the *Missouri Intelligencer*, the first newspaper published in Missouri outside of St. Louis. One of the rare, complete files of this paper is housed in the State Historical Society of Missouri.

New Mexico in the spring – his own and one headed by Major Stephen Cooper. Young Cooper believed he could keep up with Becknell because he had gained some knowledge of the southwest on a trapping expedition led by his Uncle Ben during the previous spring.[2]

Since many of his boyhood friends, including a number of Coopers and Carsons, were joining one of these expeditions, William Wolfskill felt he could no longer remain at home. He convinced his neighbor, Henry Ferril,[3] a powder-maker in Boone's Lick, that they join the Becknell company. This accomplished, Wolfskill became acquainted with another member of the group, a Tennessee trapper by the name of Ewing Young, and the two made plans to keep in contact after their arrival in New Mexico. The entire company, which numbered twenty-one, planned to depart from Arrow Rock, Missouri, and follow the now-tested route to Santa Fe. From what Wolfskill could determine, Becknell had some kind of contract to supply the Mexican government with gunpowder, a product which was then extremely scarce.[4] The arrangements must have been made during the captain's brief visit to Santa Fe in 1821.[5]

The men set out in May and had covered just a short distance toward the Arkansas River when they

[2] *Missouri Intelligencer,* Sept. 3, 1822.

[3] Ferril, "Missouri Military in the War of 1812," p. 39, states that his grandfather, Henry Ferril, founded the town of Miami, Saline County, Missouri, and that his great-uncle, Jacob Ferril, ran the ferry at Arrow Rock.

[4] Barrows, in Los Angeles *World,* Oct. 1, 1887.

encountered a band of Osage Indians. Fortunately
Auguste P. Chouteau, a member of the group who
had traded with the tribe for many years as part of
the Missouri Fur Company, was able to use his influence to save the horses and supplies. Becknell knew
that on his previous trip he had experienced great
difficulty in getting even horses over Raton Pass, and
realized that taking wagons through that mountain
gorge would be utterly impossible. He therefore
decided upon a shorter route which would take his
wagon train over more level, although more perilous,
terrain. This new route, in spite of all its hardships,
would become the route over which the majority of
travel to Santa Fe would pass for many years to
come.[6]

Becknell and his men followed the Arkansas River
to a point which would later be called "The Caches"
by Santa Fe traders. This area, located about five
miles west of modern Dodge City, received its name
from a trapping party which lost its pack animals in
the winter of 1822. The men were forced to cache
their goods and hike into Taos. These holes were
soon used as landmarks and could still be seen a
quarter of a century later. It had been a struggle to
haul the heavy wagons across the roadless country,
but now Becknell's company left the river and turned

[5] *Missouri Intelligencer,* June 17, 1823, quotes Becknell as stating that
the Mexican governor "was courteous and friendly . . . , expressed
a desire that the Americans would keep up an intercourse with that
country, and said that if any of them wished to emigrate, it would give
him pleasure to afford them every facility."

[6] R. L. Duffus, *The Santa Fe Trail* (New York, 1930), 78.

southward across the desert toward the Cimarron
River. The party's supply of water was limited to
that which could be carried in canteens, and for Billy
Wolfskill this was to be the most harrowing experience of the journey. For two days they found no
water and suffered through an almost unbearable
burning heat. Nothing was brought to their blurred
vision but mirages of lakes, streams and perhaps a
small golden city. Wolfskill and the others were
forced to cut the ears off their mules and suck the
blood. Finally, when chances of survival seemed
remote, the party came upon a buffalo which they
were able to kill. They found the animal's stomach
filled with water and one of the men commented to
Josiah Gregg years later "that nothing ever passed
his lips which gave him such exquisite delight as his
first draught of that filthy beverage." [7]

Knowing that water must be close at hand, Wolfskill, Young and some of the stronger members of the
party pushed on to the Cimarron River and returned
with water to save the lives of their weaker companions. The fact that Becknell's own journal fails to
mention the near-tragedy probably results from his
desire to emphasize the trail's advantages rather than
its faults. Becknell does admit, however, that it was
no easy task to push the wagons by hand up a number
of high and rocky cliffs.[8]

---

[7] Josiah Gregg, *Commerce of the Prairies* (Norman, 1954), 15.

[8] William Becknell's report in Archer B. Hulbert, *Southwest on the
Turquoise Trail* (Colorado Springs, 1933), 56-68. See also "The Journals
of Capt. Thomas Becknell from Boone's Lick to Santa Fe and from Santa
Cruz to Green River," in *Missouri Hist. Review,* IV (Jan. 1910), 65-84.

Both Cooper's and Becknell's expeditions had set out from Missouri in May of 1822, but that led by Stephen Cooper made much better speed because it was not encumbered by wheeled vehicles. However, Captain Becknell's efforts in getting the first wagons through that rugged country were nothing short of heroic, and for this reason he was recognized in later years as the "Father of the Santa Fe Trail." [9]

Upon their arrival in Santa Fe in the summer of 1822, the members of the company set out to explore the neighboring country for nitre, one of the essentials in their powder-making enterprise. Because the men were unable to find any or to obtain it from any other source, the party broke up and all but three or four went back to Missouri. William Wolfskill and Ewing Young were among those who remained in New Mexico. In the fall of 1822 they organized a trapping party and headed for the Pecos River, where they trapped until December.[10]

The piecing together of an accurate account of the fur trade in the Southwest involves a number of difficulties which are of little consequence in a similar account of the industry in the Northwest. The material available to the historian of the Hispanic period in the Southwest in no way compares with that provided by the journals, records, newspaper accounts, and other sources of information on fur trading activities in the Upper Missouri and Rocky Mountain region. There are several reasons for the

9 Duffus, *The Santa Fe Trail,* 78.
10 Barrows, in Los Angeles *World,* Oct. 1, 1887.

existence of this problem, although the basic one lies in the character of the business itself. The greater portion of the fur trade in the Southwest was illegal because only Mexicans could obtain licenses to trap in Mexican rivers and streams. The Mexicans, however, were not interested in trapping and left the industry without competition to the American trappers, who either had to become citizens of Mexico or conceal the real facts of what they were doing.

Another reason stems from the fact that the fur traders in the Northwest usually worked out of some sort of headquarters in Missouri, where their records and various papers were accumulated and still remain. The trappers working out of Taos and Santa Fe seldom had any permanent organization and would generally dispose of their furs and disband their party after each expedition. Few of them kept any records at all. Some information has been obtained from documents in the Archives of Mexico but here another problem joins the confusion. The Spanish method of handling foreign names, though probably sufficient for their purposes, was seldom consistent. For example, Ewing Young's name is given Julián Joon or Joaquín Joven; Ceran St. Vrain's name appears as Ceran Sambrano; John Heath as Juan Gid; James Kirker is translated into Santiago Querque; Baptiste St. Germain into Bautista Sangerma; and William Wolfskill to Guillermo Guisquiel.

The newspapers of St. Louis and other frontier settlements of Missouri announced the arrival and

departure of trapping parties for the Upper Missouri
River and also add to the information on the Northwest. When trapping was at its height in the Southwest, there were no newspapers in New Mexico to
make a similar report of their activities. And conditions of trade being as they were, it was probably
just as well. But the lack of information does not
lessen appreciably the importance of the American
fur trade in the far Southwest.

Among the prominent men who trapped in this
region were such well-known names as Jedediah
Smith, Sylvester and James Ohio Pattie, Antoine
Robidoux, Moses Carson, Jules De Mun, David
Jackson, David Waldo, Job F. Dye, Thomas Fitzpatrick and numerous others mentioned elsewhere in
this work. Dozens more could easily be included.

In January of 1823, William Wolfskill and a New
Mexican with whom he had trapped on the Pecos
River the preceding fall, set out on a trapping venture down the Río Grande to El Paso del Norte.[11]
They trapped whatever beaver they could find on the
journey down the river, but soon found the bitter
cold made it almost impossible to camp out. The
winter snows had covered the ground completely so
the two trappers decided to build a small brush hut
for protection. On the night of January 27, Wolfskill awoke to find that the New Mexican had built a
big fire at the door of the hut, but since this was

[11] Henry D. Barrows, "William Wolfskill, the Pioneer," in *Annual
Publications of the Historical Society of Southern California,* v (1902),
290.

nothing unusual, he went back to sleep. Moments later, Wolfskill was shot in the chest with a rifle ball. He first reached for his rifle but could find only the shot pouch in its place. He then stumbled out of the small hut in search of his partner.

Since the force of the ball had been slowed by passing first through his blankets and then through his right arm and left hand, Wolfskill narrowly escaped death. Assuming he had been the victim of an Indian attack and that his New Mexican companion had been killed, he started back on foot to the nearest Mexican settlement. Summoning all of his reserve strength and courage, Wolfskill began walking over the rugged and snow-covered trail to the town of Valverde, which lay at a distance of twenty-five miles. He arrived the next morning exhausted and weak from loss of blood and reported the incident to the town's alcalde.

Several hours later, much to the amazement of everyone, there appeared at the settlement of Valverde the New Mexican trapper with the report that he had been attacked by Indians and that his partner, Mr. Wolfskill, had been killed. He was naturally astonished to learn that Wolfskill had arrived before him. The New Mexican was required, much against his will, to go back with the soldiers from Valverde and show them exactly where Wolfskill had been shot. In the snow they found the footprints of the two trappers but no others; no signs of Indians were discovered. The soldiers took the New Mexican back to Valverde and kept him confined for several days until he became nearly frozen. He finally promised to show them where he had hidden the gun, and upon its discovery pretended that he had shot Wolfskill accidently, not being used to the hair-trigger of the rifle.

The New Mexican was given a hearing before the alcalde, who ordered him sent to the governor of New Mexico at Santa Fe for trial. However, his punishment was delayed and, as Wolfskill later learned, was kept going back and forth under escort between Valverde and Santa Fe until he was finally turned loose. Wolfskill could never imagine what motive his companion could have had for wanting to kill him, unless possibly it was for the sake of the old rifle. That and a few beaver traps were all Wolfskill had at the time, and these certainly did not seem of sufficient value to lead a man to murder. According to a statement later made to his son-in-law, Henry Barrows, Wolfskill believed that the loss of blood and his nearly freezing in the long tramp to the settlement saved his life. This was at a time when blood-letting was not uncommon. The rifle ball did not penetrate the breast-bone and was afterwards extracted.[12] It was fortunate for William Wolfskill that he slept with his arms folded across his chest, and was thereby spared for an eventful future in various economic activities throughout the Hispanic Southwest and in the Pacific Coast province of California.

[12] *Ibid.*, pp. 296-97. Barrows states that the account of this incident was "taken directly from Wolfskill's own lips" and could "be relied upon as absolute truth." Some members of the family felt that Wolfskill's death in later years resulted from the effects of this wound.

In August of 1823 William Wolfskill returned to
Santa Fe and remained there until December in
order to regain his strength. The town of Santa Fe,
founded in 1608, claimed a population of almost five
thousand people. Mexican rule had replaced the
Spanish flag in 1822, and from that time on commerce with the east over the Santa Fe Trail was encouraged. The way of life in this historic outpost of
the Spanish empire was relatively simple, although
there were sharp distinctions between the *gente principal* or gentry, and the *peones* or common people.
To one observer the ladies of Santa Fe were "far
more beautiful than those of the same ranks in America" and the men were "honest – perhaps more so
than those of the same class in the United States, vain
and proud of their blood. . ." [13] The architecture
of the town was plain and functional, and buildings
were made of native mud bricks smeared with a thin
mud plaster. To some the town was beautiful because
of its simplicity, but to others it appeared as "a
wretched collection of mud houses without a single
building of stone." [14]

There had not been much progress made in the
realm of social and cultural activities, but Santa Fe
was not, as Senator Thomas Hart Benton of Missouri
stated in a speech to the Senate in 1824, a capital of
people among whom all the arts were lost. It was

---

[13] Quoted from the Evansville, Indiana, *Journal,* in the *Niles National
Register,* Dec. 4, 1841.

[14] George F. Ruxton, *Ruxton of the Rockies,* ed. by LeRoy R. Hafen
(Norman, Okla., 1950), 180.

hardly as primitive as Benton's comment that there
were "no books, no newspapers," with people "cultivating the earth with wooden tools and spinning on a
stick."[15] There was, in fact, much to interest foreigners – the market-place with its exhibits of melons,
fresh fruits and baked piñon nuts; the constant gam-
bling with Mexican cards in glittering saloons or in
private homes; the religious processions complete
with pomp and pageantry; and the Mexican himself, constantly smoking his corn-husk cigarette, and
flashing his welcome smile to the American, English
or French visitor. Thus, with its governmental headquarters, its centuries-old society, and its role as cross-
roads of the Southwest, the pueblo of Santa Fe
fulfilled a larger destiny than at first glance was
apparent.

But Billy Wolfskill was restless in Santa Fe. He
gathered his few belongings together at Christmas
time and headed for Taos. Here he found his friend
Ewing Young and the two fitted out for a trapping
expedition to the headwaters of the San Juan River
and other tributaries of the Colorado. They left in
February of 1824 with a large party of trappers, but
as the men continued around the west side of the
Sierra Madre, the various members became separated
by working down different streams which suited their
individual hunting activities. Finally it was only
Wolfskill, Young and another companion, Isaac
Slover, who were still together. The three remained

---

[15] Quoted in Sabin, *Kit Carson Days*, 24.

out until beaver season was over and did not return to Taos until June. The furs which they collected on this expedition brought nearly ten thousand dollars.[16]

The Santa Fe Trail caravan which arrived in July, 1824, included eighty-one traders, one hundred and fifty-six horses and mules, twenty-five wagons and a small piece of field artillery for the purpose of fighting Indians. When the traders learned of the fur resources on the upper branches of the Colorado River, many of them immediately formed parties to trap the region. Among the members of the group returning with the caravan were Augustus Storrs, appointed American consul to Santa Fe in 1825, and M. M. Marmaduke, later governor of Missouri. Both men wrote accounts of their experiences over the trail. The caravan returned to Missouri in September with $180,000 in gold and silver and $10,000 in furs – a nice profit on an investment of about thirty-five thousand dollars.[17]

In November of 1824, Wolfskill left Taos to go south with a party led by a Captain Owens for the purpose of buying horses and mules to take to Louisiana. They bought the animals in the northwestern part of Chihuahua and drove them as far as the Presidio del Norte. Near this point the party was attacked by Indians and several of the men, including Captain Owens, were killed. The entire herd having been stampeded, the men were left on foot. However,

---

[16] Joseph J. Hill, "Ewing Young in the Fur Trade of the Far Southwest, 1822-1824," in *Oregon Historical Quarterly*, XXIV (March 1923), 19.

[17] Duffus, *The Santa Fe Trail*, 84; *Missouri Intelligencer*, Aug. 5, 1825.

some of the animals were not captured by the Indians and strayed back to the presidio where they were recovered by Wolfskill and a member of the party known as Belcher. With money left by Captain Owens, Wolfskill was able to buy some other mules and the two men started home with the animals they had collected.

Because of the danger of Indian attacks, Wolfskill and his companion thought it best to return home by way of the Mexican settlements along the Gulf. They started down by way of the Rio Grande with a man who had just come from Matamoros as the pilot of a company of French maritime traders. The men left Santa Rosa on the Sabine River in February of 1825, and in the company of some traders from Galveston Bay hoped to gain passage on a schooner for New Orleans. Failing to make connections, Wolfskill continued on alone by land to Natchitoches, Louisiana, and then booked passage on a steamer traveling up the Mississippi to St. Louis. Weary from his long journey and in poor health because of his chest wound, the young adventurer arrived at his father's home in Boone's Lick in June of 1825.[18]

William Wolfskill thus ended his first expedition into the great region of the Southwest, having been gone more than three years. During this time he had experienced the hardships of opening a new trail to Santa Fe, had been a part of trapping expeditions which penetrated the uncharted tributaries of the

[18] Barrows, in Los Angeles *World,* Oct. 1, 1887.

Colorado River on the Pacific Slope, had survived an attempt on his life, and had managed to escape from an Indian attack to make the long trek back to Missouri. For a lesser individual this might have been sufficient, but Billy Wolfskill had just begun.

Wolfskill was not content to remain at home for long. He soon left for Natchitoches where he had arranged to meet Belcher on the fourth of July of 1825. Belcher had kept the mules on the agreement that Wolfskill would then take them to the east and sell them for the benefit of Captain Owens' family, the latter being neighbors of Wolfskill's father in Boone's Lick. Belcher was not to be found at Natchitoches at the same time agreed upon, so Wolfskill traveled west to San Felipe de Austin, a distance of over three hundred miles. There he finally made contact with Belcher and took charge of the mules, which he knew would bring a good price in the southern states. These mules were the type which later became known as "Missouri mules" although they were actually of Mexican origin. Wolfskill drove his mules across Louisiana and Mississippi to Greenborough, Alabama, and there sold the animals. He decided to remain in Alabama for the winter, but in March of 1826, the young trapper-turned-mule-trader returned by way of Mobile and New Orleans to his home in Missouri. Once again in Boone's Lick, Wolfskill gave the proceeds of the sale to Captain Owens' family.[19]

---

[19] *Ibid.*

In nearby Franklin, Ewing Young, who had returned from a successful trapping and trading season
in Santa Fe,[20] was organizing a party to return to
New Mexico. Hearing news of his friend from Tennessee and remembering his profitable venture with
Young in the Southwest, Wolfskill could no longer
ignore the lure of the fur trade. In this, however, he
was not alone, for the year 1826 was especially notable for the number and size of the trapping parties
which were fitted out soon after the arrival of the
caravan from Missouri in the latter part of July of
that year. The leaders of the parties had to apply to
Governor Antonio Narbona of New Mexico for
passports to Sonora, and these were generally issued
for "trading purposes" only. Narbona soon realized
that the principal intention of these persons was
"hunting beaver on the San Francisco, Gila and
Colorado Rivers," and therefore wrote to the governor of Sonora to inform him of the size and character of the parties to whom he had issued passports.
In the letter he states that J. Williams and Sambrano
(St. Vrain) were taking twenty-odd men; that Miguel Rubidu (Robidoux) and Sylvester Pratt were
taking thirty or more; that Juan Roles (possibly
John Rowland) had eighteen in his party; and that

[20] Libro donde constan copiadas por menor las cuentas seguidas a los
estrangeros de la America del Norte que han introdusido efectos de
comercio sugetos al pago de los derechos del quince por ciento de inter-
nacion y tres por ciento de consumo en todo el presente año de 1825 en la
Aduana Nacional del Territorio de Santa Fee del Nuevo Mexico; MS no.
81, Ritch Collection, Huntington Library, San Marino, California.

Joaquin Joon (Ewing Young) had eighteen in his company.[21]

Upon their arrival in Santa Fe, Young secured the passport mentioned above, but sickness prevented his going out with the party. He hired William Wolfskill to take charge of the expedition, which had fitted out to trap the Río Gila. Among the members of the group, which originally numbered eleven, were such well-known figures as Milton Sublette, brother of the equally famous Rocky Mountain trapper William Sublette, and George Yount, a Missouri businessman who had arrived with the caravan that summer.[22] In addition they were joined by a party of five trappers which had been organized by Thomas L. Smith, later known in California as "Peg-leg Smith," and a Frenchman by the name of Maurice Le Duc.[23] These two adventurers had explored a large area of central Utah, had their horses stolen by Ute Indians, fled across the San Juan into Arizona and finally ended up by spending several days with the Moqui Indians near the Little Colorado River before returning to Taos.[24]

The party headed for the Gila River and after traveling for two to three weeks found good trapping areas. The beaver were abundant and all appeared

21 Antonio Narbona to the Governor of Sonora, Aug. 31, 1826, Archivo de Governación (Mexico), Comercio, expediente 44; copy in the Bancroft Library, University of California, Berkeley.

22 Charles L. Camp, ed., "The Chronicles of George C. Yount," in *California Historical Society Quarterly,* II (April 1923), 10.

23 "The Story of an Old Trapper. Life and Adventures of the Late Peg-Leg Smith," in San Francisco *Daily Evening Bulletin,* Oct. 26, 1866.

24 David Lavender, *Bent's Fort* (New York, 1954), 62.

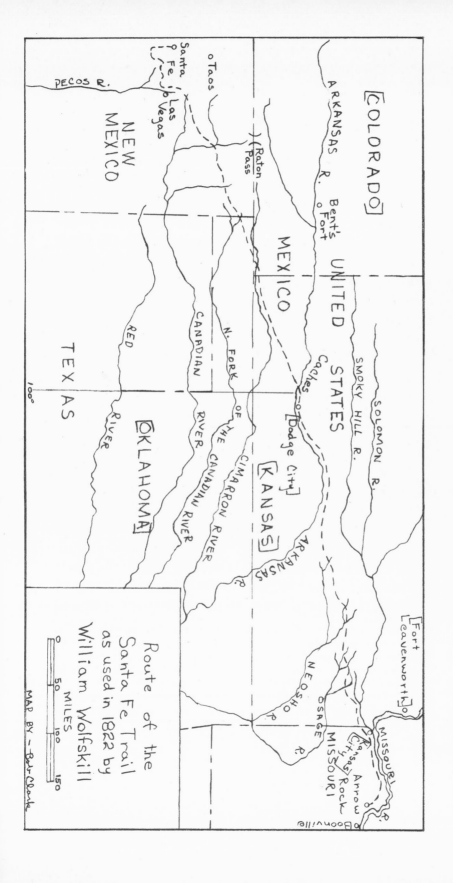

well, even with the arrival of a band of Apaches. The Indians demonstrated apparent signs of friendship and willingly shared a feast with Wolfskill and his companions. Just as they were leaving, however, one of the red men shot an arrow into an animal. This meant a declaration of hostilities. The trappers, although well-armed, did not wish to begin fighting Indians, so they decided it would be best for them to leave that part of the country. They packed their things for a hasty retreat, but Tom Smith and Milton Sublette were determined to take up their traps. While completing the task, the two men became the target for a shower of arrows and Sublette was hit in the leg. Only with the aid of Smith did he manage to escape. The members of the party, now relieved of their traps, were left with no choice but to return to Santa Fe.[25]

Ewing Young, who had meanwhile recovered, reorganized the party and set out with about thirty men for the same general area on the Gila River. Somewhere in the vicinity they picked up James Ohio Pattie, who had luckily escaped being massacred by sneaking out of Miguel Robidoux's party the year before. This self-styled hero was allowed to remain with the group.[26] They were successful in trapping without further trouble from the Apaches, but they ran into more serious difficulty with the Mexican government upon their return to Santa Fe.

[25] "The Story of an Old Trapper," in San Francisco *Daily Evening Bulletin,* Oct. 26, 1866.

[26] Joseph J. Hill, "New Light on Pattie and the Southwestern Fur Trade," in *Southwestern Historical Quarterly,* XXVI (April 1923), 253.

It all stemmed from a change in personnel in the Mexican capital while the ill-fated expedition was out in Arizona. There had always been in existence a law which prohibited foreigners from trapping beaver in Mexican territory under penalty of confiscation, but Governor Narbona, realizing there were no native Mexican trappers, thought it would be expedient to issue licenses to foreigners who would take along a certain number of Mexicans and teach them the methods of trapping. Prior to the return of Young's party, Narbona was succeeded by Manuel Armíjo who, they learned, was planning to seize their furs. To prevent this Young and Sublette stowed the furs in the house of "a wretch named Don Luis Cabeza de Vaca," on the outskirts of Santa Fe, while they attempted to obtain a trading license. However, the location of their hiding place became known and soldiers under the direction of the alcalde of Santa Fe confiscated their entire catch. Only Milton Sublette, who boldly seized his two packs and ran, was able to get to the United States with any of the furs. Ewing Young figured that he had lost $18,000 to $20,000 worth of furs to the Mexican government.[27]

Fortunately, William Wolfskill was not a member of Young's second expedition to the Gila, having gone to Sonora, Mexico, with William and Robert Carson. The Carson brothers had arrived from Missouri in the fall of 1826, leaving their sixteen-year-

[27] Gregg, *Commerce of the Prairies*, 227-28; Lavender, *Bent's Fort*, 70.

old brother Kit, or so they thought, back in Franklin. Young Kit Carson had been apprenticed to David Workman, brother of trapper William Workman of later California fame, to learn the saddler's trade. To a boy from Boone's Lick, saddle making seemed extremely dull. When he learned that his brothers were heading for Santa Fe, Kit followed on a mule and caught them a few miles out of Franklin. William, Hamilton and Robert about-faced Kit and his mule and instructed him to return home. A little way back Kit let the mule go, and joined another caravan belonging to Bent, St. Vrain and Co., and in spite of all, managed to finally arrive in Santa Fe.[28]

When William and Robert Carson joined Wolfskill's expedition to buy work-mules, mares for breeding and other horses in Sonora, they had dismissed Kit from their thoughts and eagerly looked forward to the trip to the northern parts of Mexico. They traveled to Arispe, Oposura and other towns in Sonora. Wolfskill and a partner whose name was Talbot gathered about two hundred animals and started back with them by way of Taos. Again victims of an Indian attack, they lost all but twenty-seven of the animals. With these, Wolfskill and the Carson brothers arrived at Independence, Missouri, a little before Christmas of 1826. William Wolfskill decided to spend the remainder of the winter at home, making only one short business trip to Kentucky for his father.[29]

[28] Sabin, *Kit Carson Days*, 13.
[29] Barrows, in Los Angeles *World*, Oct. 1, 1886.

3

Opening the Old Spanish Trail

We detachments steady throwing
Down the edges, through the passes,
                              up the mountains steep,
Conquering, holding, daring,
                    venturing as we go the unknown ways
Pioneers! O pioneers!
— Walt Whitman

William Wolfskill left his home in Boone's Lick, Missouri for the last time in the spring of 1828. The now seasoned adventurer made plans for his third trip westward over the Santa Fe Trail. At this point in his career, Wolfskill decided to become a trader and negotiated the purchase of a wagon and team of mules. Thus completing the necessary requisites, Wolfskill stocked his wagon with goods which he knew were in demand in New Mexico and joined a company of about one hundred wagons bound for Santa Fe. The eight-hundred-mile trail was covered without incident and the caravan received a hearty welcome in the New Mexican capital. Soon after his arrival, Wolfskill met his old friend Ewing Young who offered to purchase all of his merchandise.[1]

Wolfskill and Young discussed the business opportunities in the area and decided to proceed to nearby Taos. There the two men formed a partnership with

---

[1] Barrows, "William Wolfskill, the Pioneer," 293.

Solomon Houck, a Santa Fe trader who was willing
to provide financial backing for the purpose of fitting
out an expedition to trap in the waters of the "California Valley." [2] Young, however, concluded that it
would be more profitable to remain in Taos and
maintain a general trading business with Wolfskill
at least until the summer of 1829. The partners did
send out several parties to trap the area of the Gila
and Colorado Rivers, but these were not very successful.[3]

The Valley of Taos, located about eighty miles
north and slightly eastward of Santa Fe, was a busy
place and was second only to the capital city as a
center of activity. The small villages of San Gerónimo de Taos, San Fernando de Taos and Los Ranchos
de Taos, which lay within this fertile valley of New
Mexico, were crowded with mountain men and
traders. The valley served as a favorite gathering
place for Mexicans, Spaniards, Indians, Frenchmen
and Americans who mingled together in the village
streets. For almost ten years the mountain men had
been using Taos and Santa Fe to outfit themselves
for beaver hunting expeditions and to obtain the
necessary licenses from the Mexican government.
Here they also squandered the profits of their labors
in the numerous taverns, for Taos especially was a
"lively wintering place, and many were the fan-

2 J. J. Warner, "Reminiscences of Early California from 1831 to 1846,"
in *Annual Publications of the Historical Society of Southern California*,
VII (1907-08), 190.
3 Hill, "Ewing Young," 22.

dangoes, frolics and fights which came off." [4] Its principal industries, besides the trade in furs, robes, blankets, gunpowder and other trapper goods, consisted of the manufacture from fermented wheat of the famous "Taos lightning," and a primitive, subsistence type agriculture. Taos itself was a rural version of Santa Fe and its physical features have changed little since the epoch of the fur trade.[5]

While Ewing Young looked after the business in Taos, Wolfskill traveled the three-hundred-twenty-mile caravan trail to El Paso del Norte on the Rio Grande River. This town, which is present day Ciudad Juarez in Mexico, was the gateway to Chihuahua and central Mexico and was best known for its grape products – "Pass Brandy" and "Pass Wine." Wolfskill planned to purchase a supply of wines, brandy, panoche and similar items which he would take back to Taos in the spring of 1829.

During Wolfskill's absence a young, unemployed trapper arrived in Taos looking for work. Ewing Young consented to give the boy a job as cook when he learned that he was a friend of William Wolfskill. The boy's name was Kit Carson. Young did not feel that Kit had enough experience to accompany his trapping expeditions so, after a winter of cooking, Kit set out with a trading caravan bound for Chihuahua. After changing jobs and directions several times, the future "scout" returned to Taos with the

[4] Cardinal Goodwin, "John H. Fonda's Explorations in the Southwest," *Southwestern Historical Quarterly*, XXIII (July 1919), 40.

[5] Sabin, *Kit Carson Days,* 27-28.

remainder of one of Young's trapping parties which
had been attacked and defeated by a band of Indians.[6] When Kit delivered this unwelcome news,
Ewing Young decided to take command of his trappers in person and organized a new company of
about forty men. Armed with passports signed by
Henry Clay and the Mexican Minister in Washington, Young set out in 1829 to scour the Far West
for beaver. This time he informed young Kit Carson,
who by this time had proved to be very efficient, that
he could "come along" with the party. William
Wolfskill, having returned from El Paso, was left
behind in Taos to carry on the trading business.[7]

Because of his previous encounter with the Mexican authorities, Ewing Young thought he would
waive the formality of securing a license from that
government for trading or trapping. In order to
make it appear as though they were heading for the
United States, Young's party first traveled northward
for fifty miles to the San Luis Valley in the southern
portion of present day Colorado and then turned to
the southwest through the Navajo country to Zuñi.
From there they proceeded to the region of the Green
River and trapped in the area for several weeks. At
this point the party was divided and about half returned to New Mexico with the furs taken thus far.
The remaining eighteen, under Young's command,
set out for the Sacramento Valley in California. Kit
Carson was a member of the group which remained

6 Christopher Carson, "Kit Carson's Story as Told by Himself," MS,
n.d., Bancroft Library.   7 Hill, "Ewing Young," 23.

with Young and kept an account of the journey. He reported that they took a southerly route through Arizona "into unexplored country" although in fact they followed approximately the route taken by Juan de Oñate in 1604 and Father Francisco Garcés in 1776. They crossed the Colorado River, continued over miles of desert, and finally reached the dry Mojave River bed. Following the Mojave, the trappers eventually made their way through Cajon Pass and reached Mission San Gabriel, sometime in the early part of 1830. Because of numerous and bitter conflicts with the Apaches, Maricopas and Mojaves, their route was not one which would be immediately used by parties to California, but one which fifty years later would become a link in the Santa Fe Railroad and the general route of present U.S. Highway 66.[8]

The members of Young's party who had returned to New Mexico with the furs brought the news to William Wolfskill that his partner had gone to California. Wolfskill then began to formulate plans for his own expedition to the Pacific Coast. From the varied collection of men found in the vicinity of Taos in 1830, he selected the group which would accompany his opening of the famous route to California known as the "Old Spanish Trail."[9]

---

[8] Carson, "Kit Carson's Story," 13; Sabin, *Kit Carson Days,* 39ff.

[9] Estado que manifiesta los nombres, lugares de su nacimiento, industria o giro y edad de las personas a quienes se ha estendido carta de naturaleza, por el Gefe Politico del Territorio del Nuevo Mexico, en virtud de la autoridad que por la ley de 14 de Abril de 1828 se le confiere, desde 31 de Diciembre hasta 31 de Diciembre de 1830. Mexican Archives of New Mexico, no. 2803, Santa Fe.

Wolfskill planned to enter California through the southern part of the territory and then proceed northward to trap the beaver of the San Joaquin and Sacramento Valleys. He hoped to find Ewing Young somewhere in the latter area in order that the two parties could join together for further trapping expeditions. Wolfskill decided to delay his departure until after the trading companies from the United States arrived in Taos in July. In preparation for the trip he made a legal application for citizenship in San Gerónimo de Taos, and in a petition addressed to the *Señor Gefe Político* of the Territory of New Mexico declared as follows:

[I,] José Guillermo Wolfskill, unmarried, native of the state of *Mixuri* belonging to the United States of North America, merchant by trade and occupation, 32 years of age, resident in the jurisdiction of Taos, come before your Honor with the sole object of supporting that which is practiced in said jurisdiction of my residency by virtue of that which is provided for by the law of April 14, 1828 . . . and according to that which is fair and equitable by virtue of that which is habitually practiced, by the solemn promises which I have expressly made, and by the renunciation which I again make of any submission or obedience to whatever nation or foreign government, especially to that or those to which I have belonged, renouncing similarly all title, decoration or favor which I have obtained from whatever government, and finally by the promise that I shall support in the most lawful manner the Federal Constitution, Constituent Act and general laws of the United States of Mexico, I beg to be extended the letter of naturaliaztion which I seek and respectfully ask and beseech your Honor to grant me this favor.[10]

Wolfskill had first been required to file a lengthy

petition with the *ayuntamiento* declaring that he had been properly baptized as a Roman Catholic, was presently in good standing in his parish, and that two witnesses, D. Juan de los Reyes Martínez and D. Antonio Lucero, would attest to the fact. He also had to declare that his trade or occupation was sufficient for his maintenance, that he had renounced all foreign governments and especially that of the United States, and that he would faithfully support the government and laws of Mexico.[11]

On March 25, 1830, the "Very Illustrious Ayuntamiento of San Gerónimo de Taos meeting in regular session in the municipal hall of San Fernando," considered Wolfskill's petition and certified the information cited therein so that it could pass to the governor for issuance of the letter of naturalization. The *ayuntamiento* based its favorable recommendation on the conclusion that "from the year 1822, in which he arrived in this district, Wolfskill had wanted to become a Christian, had been converted in the jurisdiction of Taos, and, according to the local priest, had verified his conversion by having his certificate of baptism duly recorded in the parish archives." The *ayuntamiento* also concluded that the Missouri trader "had observed the duties of being a Christian, that his occupation as a merchant, carpenter or the

10 José Guillermo Wolfskill to the Governor of New Mexico, Petition for Citizenship, San Gerónimo de Taos, March 25, 1830.   Mexican Archives of New Mexico, no. 2496a, Santa Fe.

11 José Guillermo Wolfskill to the Ayuntamiento of San Gerónimo de Taos, Petition for Citizenship, March 25, 1830. Mexican Archives of New Mexico, no. 2496b, Santa Fe.

like was sufficient to provide a decent livelihood, and that his conduct in political, civil and religious matters was moderate and well tempered." In light of these facts, combined with his renunciation of all other governments and promise of obedience to the Mexican government, the *ayuntamiento* recommended that "in conformance with the demands of the decree of 1818 concerning naturalization of foreigners, we approve this lawful petition dated and signed on this day by the President and Secretary . . . Pablo Lucero and Antonio Ortiz." [12]

Now a Mexican citizen, "José Guillermo" Wolfskill made application for permission to hunt beaver within the territory of Mexico. On September 2, 1830 the Governor of New Mexico, Manuel Armíjo, granted him a license which served not only his present needs, but one which would later prove extremely useful in California. [13]

By the latter part of September, 1830, all of the necessary supplies for the journey had been purchased locally or from the recently arrived trading companies. William Wolfskill and his company of about twenty trappers prepared to depart. Sharing in the responsibility of leading the expedition was one of Wolfskill's former companions in Missouri, George C. Yount. Like the Carsons, the Coopers and the Wolfskills, the Yount family had migrated from

12 Recommendation for approval of citizenship, March 25, 1820. Mexican Archives of New Mexico, no. 2497, Santa Fe.

13 Record of Decrees, September 2, 1830. Mexican Archives of New Mexico, no. 102, Santa Fe.

North Carolina to Howard County. During the War of 1812, Jacob Yount and his five sons, including George, served with the garrison from Boone's Lick which protected Fort Cooper and vicinity from Indian attacks. After the war George married, entered into business in Franklin, and might have remained in Missouri had his savings not been stolen by a neighbor. To regain his fortune, George Yount joined the Santa Fe caravan which brought him to Santa Fe in 1826. He engaged in trapping beaver in New Mexico and the Colorado region for four years and visited the Mojave Indian Villages on two separate occasions. Some of his experiences had been in the company of Jedediah Smith in 1826[14] and Yount was as familiar with the territory to be crossed as anyone then in Taos.[15]

The exact number of participants in the expedition has not been determined with certainty because no official journal of the trip was kept. However, from various reminiscent accounts made by members of the party in later years, and from Wolfskill's overland ledger recording the financial transactions of the men in the party, it is possible to account for most of the members and to trace the progress of the journey with a fair degree of accuracy.

Wolfskill's ledger of accounts covers those which he kept in Taos prior to his departure, those kept

---

[14] A. M. Woodbury, "The Route of Jedediah Smith in 1826," in *Utah Historical Society Quarterly,* IV (April 1931), 41.

[15] LeRoy R. Hafen and Ann W. Hafen, *The Old Spanish Trail* (Glendale, Calif., 1954), 140.

during his overland expedition, and those which were active in California until early 1832.[16] The ledger, which covers the period from August, 1830, to April, 1832, includes the charges of a total of twenty-nine men, but only seventeen of these men have ledger entries during the period from September 29, 1830, to February 5, 1831, the inclusive dates of the trip from Santa Fe to California. The seventeen men who are listed in the ledger and who definitely accompanied the expedition include both Wolfskill's employees and five free trappers hired by George C. Yount. The first group included John Lewis, Ziba (Zebedia) Branch, John Ray (Rhea), Samuel Shields, David Keller, Jose Archulate (Archuleta), Manuel Mondragon, Love Hardesty, Blass Greago, Martin Cooper and Lewis Burton and those in Yount's employ were Zachariah Ham, Francisco Lafurry (Le Fourri), Alexander Branch, Batees Sangerma (Baptiste St. Germain) and Batees Garry (Bautista Guerra). It is possible that some independent members of the party made no transactions with Wolfskill during the trip and would therefore not be included in the ledger.[17]

Juan José Warner, or Jonathan Trumbull Warner as he was known in his native Connecticut, had arrived in Santa Fe early in 1830 and was on hand for

---

16 William Wolfskill, "Ledger of Accounts, 1830-1832," MS, photostat, Huntington Library. The original ledger is owned by Mrs. Marcella Wolfskill Pale-Thorpe of Los Angeles.

17 This ledger is not Wolfskill's earliest. There are several references to "amt from old book," "amt from ledger 1829" and "amt from ledger A." These earlier ledgers have not as yet been discovered.

the departure of Wolfskill's expedition. Warner, who made the trip to California in the fall of 1831 via the southern route through Yuma and San Diego, reported that Lemuel Carpenter, William G. Chard and Daniel Sill were also members of the party.[18] An additional source gives evidence that still another man, Juan Lobar, accompanied the expedition. In a communication to the alcalde of Los Angeles dated April 9, 1831, Governor Manuel Victoria refers to an order of March 6, 1831 which required all foreigners to make the necessary declarations and secure a bond signed by a Mexican citizen. The eight persons specifically named were Franco Le Fourri, Bautista St. Germain, Bautista Guerra, Zacarias Ham, Francisco Zebedia Branch, Luis Burton, Samuel Shields and Juan Lobar.[19] The last named may possibly have been John Lewis, but if not he was most likely a member of the Wolfskill party as were the first seven, even though his name, like those mentioned by Warner, was not entered in the ledger.

Wolfskill's ledger records both the charges made for items bought during the journey and the credits given for wages and beaver skins turned in. Some of the men listed in the ledger book prior to the departure of the expedition in September include such famous fur traders as Ceran St. Vrain, "Old Bill" Williams, "Peg-leg" Smith, Nathaniel Pryor and

---

[18] J. J. Warner, et al., *An Historical Sketch of Los Angeles County* (Los Angeles, 1876), 35.

[19] Manuel Victoria to the Alcalde of Los Angeles. Archives of California, *Departmental Records*, IX, pp. 95-96, Bancroft Library.

Richard Laughlin. The wages paid by Wolfskill to his employees were not always on the same basis. For example, David Keller is credited as receiving $91.93¾ for service from Taos to California, while José Archuleta was paid $21.00 for 3½ months service @ $7 per month (this must have been after deductions). Blass Greago received wages of $8.00 per month for ten months' service. Others, such as Love Hardesty and Martin Cooper, liquidated their indebtedness to Wolfskill by crediting their services to the account.

These wages were paid in addition to supplied food. Some flour was packed on the animals, and four "beeves" provided by Wolfskill were driven along for food. Yount and the free trappers who shared in this meat were each charged "To his part of 4 beeves $2.25." When the beeves were gone and the party resorted to horse meat, the account book shows a charge against each independent "To his part of 2 horses, $4.50." Alexander Branch is shown to have also provided food as his account is credited with $38.00 for "Ham and Wolfskill's board" and with $19.00 for boarding Samuel Shields.[20]

Although a large share of Wolfskill's business in Taos had been in whiskey, the most popular being "Taos Lightning" selling for 75¢ per pint, all such entries in the ledger ceases on October 1. Apparently Wolfskill took no whiskey with him on the trip –

20 Frederick W. Hodge, "Pioneers and Prices," in *Historical Society of Southern California Quarterly*, XXVIII (September 1946), 99-101.

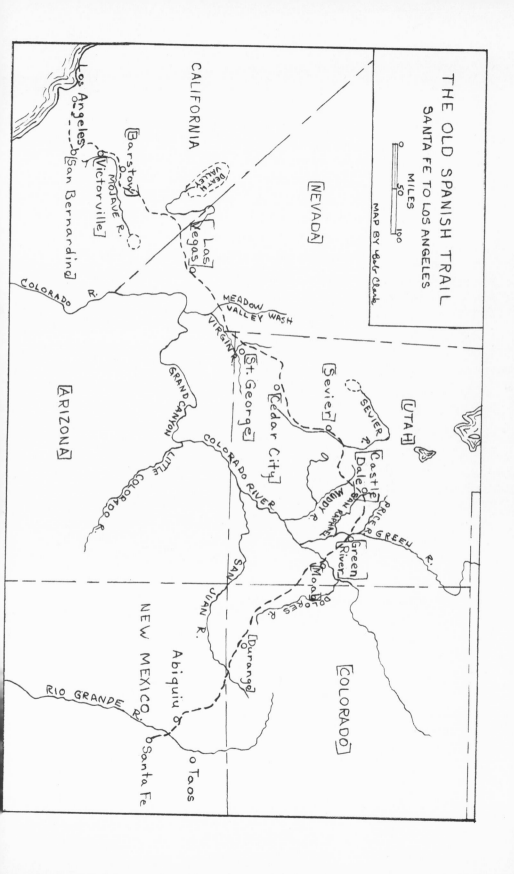

THE OLD SPANISH TRAIL
SANTA FE TO LOS ANGELES

MILES
0   50   100

MAP BY Bob Clarke

perhaps as the result of previous experience. Some of
the more typical items charged during the journey
included tobacco and gunpowder, both at $1.50 per
pound; lead @ 50¢ per pound; gun flints @ 3¢ each;
"strans" of beads used as trading items from 25¢ to
75¢ each; knives generally at $1.00 each; combs @
50¢ each; and shirts at prices ranging from $3.00 to
$6.00 apiece. Francisco Le Fourri paid $20.00 for a
"rifle gun" and George Yount was charged $15.00
for a rifle, $6.00 for a shotgun and $15.00 for a "rifle
gun." Ziba Branch evidently preferred top quality
as his "rifle gun" cost him $75.00. In addition to
food, blankets and other necessities, the members of
the expedition indulged in a few luxury items such
as jews-harps @ 25¢; handkerchiefs @ $1.50; awls
@ 12½¢, as well as trade in goods such as linen,
calico, silk stockings and vermillion. Alexander
Branch and José Archuleta each purchased shoes @
$3.00 per pair. The free trappers were given a credit
of $5.00 for each beaver skin turned in during the
trip.[21]

The route which Wolfskill's party followed after
its departure from Taos as described in later accounts
by several of the participants and by various others
on hearsay evidence can be generally traced. William
Wolfskill's own statement, which his son-in-law
Henry Barrows faithfully recorded, is the most suc-
cinct, although it may have been edited by Mr.
Barrows:

[21] Hafen and Hafen, *Old Spanish Trail,* 141.

Last of Sept., 1830, the party, with Mr. Wolfskill at its
head, left Taos for this then far off Territory of California.
They came by a route farther north than that usually adopted
by the Spaniards in traveling between California and New
Mexico – their object being to find beaver. They struck the
Colorado just below the mouth of the Dolores, at the head of
the "Great Cañon," where they crossed; entering the Great
American Basin, striking the Sevier; thence southward to the
Rio Virgin, which they followed down to the Colorado;
thence descending the Colorado to the Mojave; where they
hoped to obtain some provisions of which they were in want,
and also to find beaver. From there they took across to the
sink of the Mojave River, through the Cajon Pass to San
Bernardino, and finally to Los Angeles, where they arrived
in February, 1831.[22]

Although some sections of the Wolfskill trail cannot be determined with certainty, the majority is
subject to little doubt. Passing first through the
pueblo of Abiquiú, "where they purchased several
fine bulocks" to be driven along for meat,[23] the men
followed the Chama River northward to Horse Lake
and then traveled in a westerly direction to the San
Juan River. Whether the town of Archuleta on that
river was named for José Archuleta of the Wolfskill
party is not known, but it would have been in that
vicinity that the men struck the San Juan and followed it to its junction with Los Pinos Creek. Going
northward along the Los Pinos for a few miles, they
then turned west and cut across to the Animas River,
passing a few miles south of what is now Durango,

22 Henry Barrows, in Wilmington *Journal,* Oct. 20, 1866.
23 Rev. Orange Clark, "Chronicles of George C. Yount," MS, 1855, p. 3,
Bancroft Library.

Colorado. Bearing northwest, the party crossed the Mancos River near its headwaters and reached the Río Dolores near the present town of Dolores, Colorado.

Traveling northwest down the Dolores, the Wolfskill expedition crossed the Colorado River north of present day Moab, Utah, passed westward over Salt Wash and reached the Green River near today's town of the same name on U.S. highway 50. Crossing the Green and continuing in a northwesterly direction, the group paralleled the San Rafael River to the vicinity of what is now Castle Dale, and then turned southwest to cross the mountains near Salina Canyon and reach the Sevier River.

According to George Yount, who related his experiences to a Rev. Orange Clark in California in 1855,[24] they encountered few Indians until reaching the Sevier River. At that point, however, they came upon a tribe of Utah Indians assembled for the public funeral of their chief. The Indians remembered Yount from his previous expeditions into their country while trapping beaver and despite Yount's protests to the contrary, accepted him as leader of the expedition. Wolfskill insisted that his friend act as chief in order to place the group in a better bargaining position. Yount won the tribe's confidence by presenting them with gifts of knives, tobacco, beads, awls and vermillion. The Indians in turn gave the trappers permission to travel through the country and to "hunt and trap in all the territory of the great

---

[24] *Ibid.,* 1.

Eutau nation." Yount completed the ceremony with
some high-sounding propaganda about the powerful
nation of the United States which was headed by the
"Great Father at Washington." He told them that
not only was the president equipped with mighty
rifles, big cabins and many braves, but that he was

> . . . The vice regent and son of the Great Spirit who
> rolls the sun; whose pipe when smoking makes the clouds;
> whose big gun makes the thunder; and whose rifle bullets and
> glittering arrows make the red lightning.[25]

Yount continued with his speech until the Indians
bowed down before him, and then as a token of
tolerance he gathered some dirt from under his foot
and sprinkled it on their heads. To complete the
drama Yount ordered Wolfskill to raise each Indian
and bid him to kiss his rifle out of respect for the
"Great Father at Washington." The ceremony completed, Yount gave the signal for the distribution of
the gifts, which was really the chief object of their
regard and for which they would swear temporary
allegiance to almost anything.

The trappers stayed until the funeral was over and
noted that all the clothes, utensils, weapons, animals
and servants of the deceased chief were collected and
burned on his funeral pyre. After witnessing this
spectacle they decided it was time to move on and so
continued along the Sevier River until they passed
Otter Creek. Here they evidently took the wrong
turn at one of the branches of the Sevier and instead

---

25 Camp, "Chronicles of George C. Yount," 38ff.

of passing through Bear Valley to Little Salt Lake, they found themselves bogged down in deep snow on a high plateau. George Yount recalled that on that strip of table land they encountered the worst storm they had ever experienced.

> During several days no one ventured out of camp. There they lay embedded in snow, very deep, animals and men huddled thick as possible together, . . . having spread their thick and heavy blankets and piled bark and brush wood around and over them. . .[26]

They also covered themselves with beaver skins and by these methods were able to survive the snow storm which finally ended with several hours of rain and then a piercing cold which transformed the ground into a thick crust of ice.

Yount and Wolfskill took advantage of the clear spell to climb a nearby peak to try to determine their location. At this point Wolfskill gave up his previous plan to take a northerly course over the Sierras. The bitter cold, the scarcity of food and the "demoralization and disorganization which had seized his motley and dissatisfied company" convinced him that they should turn southward.[27] From their look-out point the two men agreed that they must continue to the upper waters of the Sevier instead of taking "the right hand route" up Clear Creek Fork as Jedediah Smith had done in 1826 and 1827. They had become stalled in the snow probably on the plateau in the vicinity of Panguich.

[26] *Ibid.,* 39.
[27] Warner, "Reminiscences of Early California," 191.

The route of descent from this tableland is not certain, but from a later statement made by Ziba Branch that they "killed their last ox near Little Salt Lake,"[28] it can probably be assumed that they came out of the mountains by the canyon that emerges by Paragoonah and near Little Salt Lake. This canyon subsequently became part of the regular course of the Old Spanish Trail. From Little Salt Lake, Wolfskill and his men struck southward again to the Santa Clara River and followed it to its junction with the Virgin River. Going down the Virgin they crossed the northwest corner of what would become the present state of Arizona, and soon reached the Colorado River at what is now Lake Mead and Hoover Dam. Although the accounts vary slightly at this point, it seems likely that they followed the Colorado River south to the Mojave Indian Villages near modern Needles, California.

Ziba Branch stated that they continued along the Red (Colorado) River, until they reached the Mojaves, and described them as a "treacherous tribe of Indians, who, however, treated them kindly and gave them bread, which was made of pounded corn and baked in the ashes."[29] Branch actually did not learn that the Indians were "treacherous" until later years. He recalled that they also were given dried pumpkins and some small white beans. The trappers stayed in the villages for two days and traded such items as red

[28] F. H. Day, "Sketches of the Early Settlers of California: Ziba Branch," in *The Hesperian*, II (October 1859), 337-39.
[29] *Ibid.*, 338.

cloth, knives and other trinkets for food. Although "they were a little apprehensive of an attack by the Indians," they finally departed in safety and set out westward across the desert to the Mojave River. Traveling through Cajon Pass, the expedition reached the ranch of Antonio María Lugo on February 5, 1831.[30]

Wolfskill's ledger indicates that some of the accounts were settled at Lugo's ranch and here some charges for whiskey were again entered. Both William Wolfskill and George Yount wanted very much to visit the Mission San Gabriel and particularly to talk with the (head) priest Father José Bernardo Sánchez, but according to Yount their "total ignorance of the spirit and customs of the country filled them with a thousand misgivings." They were certain that with their rude buckskin garb and rough personal appearance they could hardly expect much of a reception even if they gained admittance. The two trappers finally decided to call upon the father anyway and much to their surprise were given a most cordial reception.

Father Sánchez informed them that "their scrupulous honesty had preceded them there" and alluded to their reputations as satisfactory evidence that they were worthy of his hospitality. The priest fed them a hearty meal and offered sufficient lodging for the entire party. Wolfskill and Yount returned to Lugo's ranch to collect the men, and the entire group returned to the mission for a much needed and appre-

---

[30] Wolfskill, "Ledger of Accounts, 1830-32."

ciated rest. Because of the hardships of the journey
plus the exposure to the cold, even the normally
hardy trappers were glad to spend the next two weeks
enjoying the benefits of California hospitality.[31]

At this juncture Wolfskill made an important decision. The season was too far advanced for trapping
beaver on the San Joaquin River and besides, he had
heard some reports that a small animal called a sea
otter abounded on the coast and had been responsible
for some lucrative profits. After some consideration
and investigation, Wolfskill decided to send the
trappers which he had hired, back to New Mexico
with his equipment, and try his luck for one year with
the furry sea otters. The other members of the group
who also preferred to remain were Yount, Burton,
Rhea, Cooper, Shields, and Branch. After settling
all the accounts Wolfskill was "left without means or
resources and a heavy debt in New Mexico" [32] but
with an optimistic outlook toward his future in
California.

The word spread almost at once that the trail over
which Billy Wolfskill had led his men was definitely
a new and more desirable route from New Mexico
to California.

In contrast to the sometimes vague and circuitous
routes of his predecessors, Wolfskill charted a track
which traversed the entire distance across the Great
Basin and led directly into southern California.[33]

---

31 Camp, "Chronicles of George C. Yount," 45.
32 Barrows, "William Wolfskill, the Pioneer," 295.
33 Gloria Griffen Cline, *Exploring the Great Basin* (Norman, 1963),
165.

Explorers and fur traders such as Father Garcés and Fathers Domínguez and Escalante in 1776, Jedediah Smith in 1826-27, Ewing Young in 1829 and Antonio Armíjo in 1829-30 had followed parts of the same trail, but to Wolfskill belonged the honor of having marked the first route feasible for wagon trains which covered the entire distance from Taos to the Pacific. Jedediah Smith's trail had passed through a region too arid to provide water and forage, and the routes of Young and Armíjo were more difficult for trading caravans. Wolfskill's path was called the "Old Spanish Trail" because it was considered to be a continuation of a trail used by the Spaniards since the time of Don Juan María de Rivera's expedition of 1765 to the Utah Indian country. In reality, however, it was a new route discovered during the Mexican period.

Several of the members of Wolfskill's party, after reaching California, advantageously disposed of their woolen blankets, called *serapes* or *fresadas,* to the rancheros in exchange for mules. These blankets were typical of the region of New Mexico and were frequently used by the fur traders and other travelers out of Santa Fe. They were very thick and almost impervious to water. The Californians were immediately impressed with their quality. At the same time, the mules of California were much larger and of finer form than those used in the Missouri and Santa Fe trade. Their appearance in New Mexico caused quite a sensation, especially when it was learned that they had been received in trade for blankets. Juan José Warner later wrote that out of the bargain made by Wolfskill's men "there sprang up a trade, carried on by means of caravans or pack animals between the two sections of the same country, which flourished for some ten or twelve years." [34] On the other hand, a more recent source states that these trappers should not be thought of as having begun the caravan trade over the Old Spanish Trail because two months after Wolfskill's arrival in California "30 men from New Mexico, *merchants in wool,* bringing passports" appeared in Los Angeles. Since these businessmen apparently had no other purpose in going to California except to trade merchandise for mules, their transactions were those which actually began the new commerce.[35]

The Wolfskill trail did, however, become the route for the regular caravans during the 1830's and 40's even though it was a difficult one and dry in many places. The Mexicans used it more from tradition than because of its facilities. Other and better routes were known to exist further south, but during this period Wolfskill's Old Spanish Trail was the most famous.[36]

[34] Warner, *Historical Sketch of Los Angeles County,* 33.

[35] Eleanor F. Lawrence, "Mexican Trade between Santa Fe and Los Angeles 1830-1848," in *California Historical Society Quarterly,* x (March 1931), 27-29.

[36] Robert G. Cleland, *History of California: The American Period* (New York, 1923), 83.

4

The Mountain Man Settles Down

Here build your homes for good, establish here,
these areas entire, lands of the Western shore,
We pledge, we dedicate to you.

— Walt Whitman

El Pueblo de Nuestra Señora la Reina de Los Angeles by 1831 had become a fairly sizable community. It had already gained the reputation as a center of revolution and boiling pot for political intrigue.[1] The constant turmoil, however, had the disadvantage of standing in the way of civic progress. The population of California's second-oldest town consisted of about two hundred Spanish and Mexican families with a scattering of *Yanquis* who had come with trading ships or, more recently, come overland from the fur-trading country.[2]

Don Juan Temple had opened a general merchandise store and Don Abel Stearns was the leading trader of the pueblo. Richard Laughlin, who had arrived from New Mexico with Sylvester and James Ohio Pattie's expedition in 1828, had established himself as a carpenter; and Nathaniel Pryor, also of the Patties' famous trek, divided his time between silversmithing and otter hunting. Pryor was also a

---

[1] Hubert H. Bancroft, *History of California* (7 vols., San Francisco, 1886-90), III, p. 269.
[2] *Ibid.,* 632.

warehouse keeper for Abel Stearns. Samuel Prentice, a native of Rhode Island and a former sailor on the brig "Danube," decided to settle in Los Angeles after his ship was wrecked on the Pacific coast in 1830.[3]

After the members of his trapping party had gone their separate ways, William Wolfskill, together with George Yount, decided to associate himself with Pryor and Laughlin, both of whom he had known in New Mexico, and with Samuel Prentice, because of his boating skill, in an enterprise to build a vessel in which to hunt sea otter. Sea otter at this time were plentiful on the coast of both Alta and Baja California as well as on the adjacent islands.[4]

This venture was made possible entirely through a confusion of Spanish terms. As has been stated, Wolfskill had obtained letters of naturalization from the Mexican authorities before leaving New Mexico in order to obtain a license to hunt beaver in Mexican territory. It was a provincialism of New Mexico to use the word *"nutria"* instead of *"castor"* for beaver. The first was the Spanish word for otter and the latter that for beaver. In California the two words were correctly used, and therefore the license which Wolfskill had obtained from the Governor of New Mexico authorized him to hunt *nutria* (otter) throughout the jurisdiction of Mexico.[5]

Upon the presentation of his license to the author-

3 *An Illustrated History of Los Angeles County, California* (Chicago, 1889), 114.

4 Barrows, "William Wolfskill, the Pioneer," 291.

5 Warner, "Reminiscences of Early California," 192.

ities of California, they hesitated and for a time demurred to the power of the governor of New Mexico to grant a license which should be valid beyond the limits of the territory over which he was governor.[6] Governor Manuel Victoria wrote a letter on February 19, 1831 to the alcalde of Los Angeles, Vicente Sánchez, expressing his sentiments that "Guillermo Wolfskill no debe pescar en California sino en Sonora donde obtuvo licencia" (William Wolfskill should not "fish" in California but in Sonora where he obtained the license).[7] But because the officials in California had as little knowledge of New Mexico and its people as the latter had of California and the sea otter, they did not choose to present this issue with the officers of a sister territory.

They could not, however, dispute the object for which the license was issued, because it was plainly written over the sign manual of the governor and under the great seal of New Mexico that Mr. Wolfskill might hunt and catch *nutria*. The license was therefore recognized as good and valid.[8] Under this authority, William Wolfskill was able to extend his hunt over the ocean and capture sea otter, although foreign residents of California, even if married to native Californians, were not allowed to engage in this business.

[6] *Ibid.,* 193.

[7] Manuel Victoria to Vicente Sánchez, Feb. 19, 1831. *Departmental Records,* IX, p. 92, Bancroft Library.

[8] Warner, "Reminiscences of Early California," 192; George W. and Helen P. Beattie, *Heritage of the Valley* (Pasadena, 1939), 27.

Wolfskill and his partners traveled to Mission San Gabriel in order to solicit the help of their friend Father Sánchez. The priest willingly offered his assistance and assigned some of the mission's Indian laborers to the project. The men journeyed to the San Bernardino mountains in the early part of the summer of 1831 to cut timber and saw planks for the proposed vessel. The cut timber was then conveyed to San Gabriel on clumsy ox-drawn *carretas* and there worked into the necessary forms. The construction of the ship was directed by a famous early resident Joseph Chapman, an apprenticed ship-builder originally from Boston. Chapman had arrived in California in 1818 after being impressed into the service of the notorious pirate Hipolite Bouchard during the Frenchman's brief stay in Hawaii. Chapman was captured in Monterey, taken as a prisoner to Los Angeles, but later released as a result of his unwilling part in the attack. The resourceful American soon became a citizen and married María Guadalupe Ortega of the Refugio Rancho in Ventura County. After the ship was completely finished, Chapman had it dismantled so that it could be carried to the harbor at San Pedro, reassembled and launched.[9]

The schooner weighed about sixty tons and was about seventy feet in length. According to Juan José Warner, the ship was named "Refugio" by Father Sánchez, but according to Alfred Robinson, who was present at the time the vessel was launched in 1831,

---

[9] Bancroft, *History of California,* II, p. 362.

it was named "Guadalupe" after Chapman's wife.[10] It is possible that they followed the old Spanish tradition of giving a ship an official name and then calling it by a nickname.

Wolfskill and his party left San Pedro in January of 1832 and proceeded along the coast as far south as the island of Cedros. In the following summer they returned and hunted along the coast northward to San Luis Obispo and about the islands south of Point Conception. As they were not particularly successful in this venture, this was the only trip they made with the ship. It was afterwards sold to Captain William S. Hinckley who sailed her to the Sandwich Islands.[11]

Wolfskill's former partner Ewing Young was also engaged in sea otter hunting during the summer of 1832. After trapping beaver in the San Joaquin Valley, Young had returned to Santa Fe in the spring of 1831 to organize another expedition to trap the region between Santa Fe and California. Upon his return to New Mexico, Ewing Young entered into partnership with his friend David Waldo and the Rocky Mountain fur trader David Jackson. Young and a party of eleven men departed for California in September of 1831 and headed southward along the Gila River

---

[10] Warner, "Reminiscences of Early California," 192, and Barrows, "William Wolfskill, the Pioneer," 293, affirm that the vessel was named *Refugio;* Alfred Robinson, *Life in California* (San Francisco, 1891), 132, gives the name as *Guadalupe*. Bancroft in his Marine List (*History of California,* III, p. 382) lists the *Guadalupe* as weighing 60 tons, built by Joseph Chapman and launched at San Pedro in 1831.

[11] Barrows, "William Wolfskill, the Pioneer," 293. Samuel Prentice continued to hunt sea otter and eventually died on Catalina Island in 1865.

route. Among those traveling with the Tennessee trapper was Juan José Warner, and as the men completed the final leg of their journey, Warner would unknowingly pass over the site of his future ranch in the Valley of San José. They reached Los Angeles in December.

In the spring of 1832, Young, Warner and some native Californians were aided by Father Sánchez in securing a vessel for hunting sea otter. Like Wolfskill, they met with little success, and after numerous spills into the surf, Ewing Young decided to return to beaver trapping. He led an expedition which, according to Warner, took them from Los Angeles clear up to the Oregon country and back south again to San Bernardino by the end of 1833. Young then purchased a herd of horses with his furs and in the summer of 1834 drove them northward to the Columbia River, where he finally decided to settle down. He returned to California several times but only as a trader in mules and cattle. Ewing Young's death in the Willamette Valley in 1841 created a significant problem with regard to the disposition of his estate, which included six hundred cattle. Since there existed no other government but the rule of Dr. John McLaughlin of the Hudson's Bay Company, his property was handled according to the laws of New York. This occasioned the appointment of a committee to adopt a constitution and code of laws, and the first step was taken toward establishing a government for the Oregon settlement.[12]

---

[12] Bancroft, *History of California*, II, p. 600; III, pp. 174-75.

Since William Wolfskill had experienced a similar failure in sea otter hunting, he decided to try his luck in some other business venture – perhaps something more substantial. He presented his naturalization papers to the alcalde of Los Angeles on September 21, 1833, and indicated that he planned to remain in the pueblo.[13] Apparently he still planned to hunt sea otter because on the same date he applied for permission to continue that activity for six more months.[14] Governor José Figueroa granted his request on October 9, 1833, but there is no evidence that Wolfskill made further use of his hunting privilege.[15]

Sometime during the year 1833, Wolfskill, the "yanqui" trapper, bought a small tract of land containing some grape vines, settled down, and "devoted himself to unremitting labor." [16] He entered into a common-law marriage with Los Angeles born María de la Luz Valencia, daughter of Ignacio Valencia and María Luisa Varela de Valencia. On November 18, 1833, Wolfskill's first child, a daughter whom the couple named María Susana, was baptized in the Plaza Church.[17] Just over a year later, a second child,

---

[13] Hubert H. Bancroft, "Biographical Scraps: William Wolfskill," MS, p. 3, Bancroft Library.

[14] J. Guillermo Wolfskill to José Figueroa, Los Angeles, Sept. 21, 1833. *Departmental State Papers*, III, p. 173, Bancroft Library.

[15] José Figueroa to José Guillermo Wolfskill, Santa Barbara, Oct. 9, 1833. *Ibid.,* 175.

[16] J. J. Warner, "Wm. Wolfskill, the Pioneer," in San Francisco *Daily Alta California,* Oct. 12, 1866.

[17] Libro primero de Bautismos desde Marzo 4 de 1826 hasta Dic. 24 1848, Acta 398, p. 85. Iglesia de Nuestra Señora de Los Angeles, California, Archives.

son Timoteo, was also baptized in the church of "Nuestra Señora de Los Angeles.[18]

In order to support his family, Wolfskill called upon a trade learned during his youth in Missouri and entered the carpenter and joiner business in the growing pueblo. Within a short time he was kept steadily employed fulfilling contracts for houses and fences, digging wells, and working at the carpenter's bench for daily wages.[19] Among the houses which he built was a famous one-story adobe building on the Calle Principal (Main Street) contracted for by ranchero-merchant Isaac Williams. This building would serve as headquarters for Governor Pío Pico when Los Angeles was temporarily made the capital of Alta California in 1845, as headquarters for the American occupation forces under Captain Archibald H. Gillespie during the Mexican War, and later, with considerable remodeling, as the Bella Union Hotel, "the finest hotel south of San Francisco.[20]

The secularization of the missions between 1834 and 1836 brought about numerous changes in the Los Angeles area. Most of the vast holdings in land of Mission San Gabriel and Mission San Fernando were open to private claim, and much of the land was granted to those individuals closest to the governor. The missions themselves became parish churches and the Franciscan fathers were replaced

---

18 *Ibid.*, Acta 489, p. 109.

19 Warner, "Wm. Wolfskill, the Pioneer."

20 Los Angeles *Star*, June 26, 1870.

by secular clergy. Many of the local Indians, now suddenly removed from the security of mission life and unable to cope with many of the ordinary problems of existence, flocked into the pueblo to create a multitude of problems for the alcalde and other officials. At the same time an increasing number of Americans were arriving to take advantage of land opportunities which would surpass any they had known in the United States, and for this reason would soon become citizens of Mexico. The population of Los Angeles was becoming extremely heterogeneous.

The first official census of the district, entitled "Padron de la Ciudad de Los Angeles y su Jurisdicción Año 1836" lists the dwelling place, age, occupation, marital status, and national origin of the 1,675 non-Indian residents, and indicates that there were 553 Indians living in *rancherías*. Out of the fifty persons listed as foreigners, twenty-nine were Americans while the rest were Europeans. Among Wolfskill's neighbors were his former sea otter hunting associates, Nathaniel Pryor, Richard Laughlin and Samuel Prentice. Other prominent Americans included John T. Warner, just twenty-six years old, John Temple, Abel Stearns, John Marsh, Lemuel Carpenter,[21] Moses Carson, John Rhea, William Chard, Isaac Graham and more. Some of the European residents were Johannes Gronigen, a German listed as Juan Domingo, Hugo Reid from Scotland,

---

[21] Carpenter's first name is listed in the census and in other Los Angeles archival records as Samuel; both Henry Barrows and J. J. Warner, who knew Carpenter personally, give his name as Lemuel.

Jordan Pacheco and Manuel D'Olivera from Por-
tugal, Louis Bouchet and Jean Louis Vignes from
France and several from England, Ireland, Canada,
Norway, Italy and Africa. Wolfskill was listed as
"Esten Guillmo Wolfskil" age thirty-eight, a property owner and laborer, married, and a native of the
United States. His name was followed by "Luz
Valencia, 30 . . . Juan Je [Timoteo] Wolfskil,
1," and "Suzanne Wolfskil, 2." There was a total of
603 men, 421 women and 651 children under twelve
years of age living in Los Angeles.[22]

The frequent visits of Boston ships to the ports of
California provided local residents with many of the
luxury items and manufactured goods from the east
coast. Much of this trade was carried on directly
between the ship captains and Californians without
the services of customs officials. Smuggling was almost considered a necessity. The importation of
furniture, ready-made suits and dresses, and a variety
of silk and cotton cloth thus made added comforts
possible, and increased business activity in Los Angeles. New homes were built and existing homes
extended in size. The arrival of pack-train caravans
from Santa Fe during the 1830's and 40's brought
manufactured goods to be traded for horses and
mules, and Californians could get just about anything
they wanted. Life in Los Angeles was indeed cosmo-
politan and old-time residents were beginning to feel

22 J. Gregg Layne, "The First Census of the Los Angeles District," in
Historical Society of Southern California Quarterly, XVIII (June 1936),
99ff.

threatened by the influx of so many foreigners. Ten years later their fears would not be in vain.

Wolfskill continued to work as a carpenter, but tried to devote as much time as possible to the cultivation of his small vineyard. He finally decided that he needed the piece of land adjacent to his present property in order to plant some additional vines, and try out some experiments with other plants. On February 4, 1836, "Guillermo Wolfskill" as a citizen and resident of Los Angeles, filed a petition with the *ayuntamiento* which declared as follows:

> That for thirteen years I have lived under the Government of Mexico, six of which I have spent in this Territory, and declare that I have supported myself as a result of my personal occupation; in order to continue in it, I need a piece of land to cultivate and for this purpose I beg to be granted a piece of land which is contiguous (on three sides) to that which I bought from Sr. Maximo Valenzuela.
>
> If this piece which I request is not occupied, I ask that it be conceded to me with the corresponding right of possession, swearing that I ask it with good intention and because of need. . .[23]

A commission headed by Abel Stearns, by then a prosperous store-keeper and merchant in good standing with governmental officials,[24] was named by the *ayuntamiento* to investigate the property. Their decision as to whether or not it should be conceded to Wolfskill was favorable and on February 20, 1836, Don Guillermo was granted possession of the land

---

[23] Petition to the Ayuntamiento, Feb. 4, 1836. *Los Angeles Archives*, I, p. 255.
[24] *Ibid.*, 256.

"consisting of 350 *varas*[25] adjacent to the lands of Citizen Antonio Reyes; 540 *varas* adjacent to the old course of the river; 366 *varas* adjacent to unimproved land; and 540 *varas* adjacent to the highway running north 25 degrees to the west."[26] On February 25 he petitioned for 300 additional *varas* lying to the south of this property and was granted the same on April 26.[27] During this time Wolfskill also negotiated for the purchase from Eduardo Hernández of a small house "con puerta y una cosina" (with door and a kitchen) situated between the houses of Don Bacilio and Don Antonio Valdéz on the Calle Real. The deed of sale dated May 14, 1836, listed the "just price and true value" of the unfurnished house at one hundred pesos.[28]

In the spring of 1836 John Rhea, one of the trappers who had accompanied Wolfskill on the trek to California, decided to return to the East. He had kept a saloon, a billiard room and a small grocery store in Los Angeles for a few years, but apparently preferred to free himself of the responsibility. He was still only twenty-five years old. Rhea sold his property to Wolfskill who, on June 26, 1836, paid four and one-half pesos for a license allowing him to operate a saloon and billiard parlor for three months.

---

[25] One *vara* was equal to approximately thirty-three inches.

[26] Abel Stearns to Guillermo Wolfskill, Feb. 20, 1836. *Los Angeles Archives,* I, p. 260.

[27] *Ibid.,* 338.

[28] Deed of Sale, Eduardo Hernández to Guillermo Wolfskill, May 14, 1836 (witnessed by Tiburcio Tapia and Narciso Botello). Lewis Wolfskill Papers, MS 54, Huntington Library.

From the various renewals of the license, it seems that "Don Guillermo Wosquil" maintained the establishment for at least two years.[29]

Wolfskill's primary interest remained, however, in agriculture. Now that he had sufficient land to meet his needs and a house which would serve as a temporary dwelling, he devoted more time to experimentation with different methods of planting grape vines. He also studied the possibilities for distilling grape brandy. After his many years of fur trading, hunting and working at odd jobs, the "Kentucky trapper" had finally entered upon a vocation which he would pursue without interruption and with considerable success until his death in 1866. As he acquired additional land, Wolfskill cultivated a wide variety of other plants, especially citrus fruits, and investigated means for the commercial production of wine.

Unlike many of his neighbors, William Wolfskill preferred to remain aloof from certain of the political activities of the province. It is possible that the demands of his work prevented his taking an active part, or that he believed his participation was not really necessary. Wolfskill was willing to serve with those who made up the official guard of the city,[30]

---

[29] Receipts of the Ayuntamiento, 1836-1844. *Los Angeles Archives, Translations,* III, p. 47ff. The billiard table was made in Los Angeles by John Fitzpatrick, a cabinet-maker from England.

[30] List of the Individuals who shall form the Guard of this City, prepared by Abel Stearns and Bacilio Valdez, Feb. 17, 1836. *Ibid.,* 151. There were 304 members listed with place of residence and page on which they appeared in the census of 1836.

but when it involved revolutionary activities, he generally stayed on the sidelines. At last, however, an incident occurred which roused even Wolfskill from the quiet of his ranch and forced him to enter the policy of action adopted by many of his neighbors.

In the spring of 1836 the particularly vicious murder of Domingo Feliz had been committed by pueblo residents Gervacio Alipáz and his mistress, the victim's wife, María del Rosario Villa. The parties to the homicide were apprehended with little delay and were placed in the local jail; but since there was no civil court or authority in California invested with the power to execute the sentence of death, further legal action was halted.[31] A number of citizens began to complain that the pair would not receive the punishment which they "deserved" and felt that some kind of direct action should be taken. Several of these individuals held a meeting at the home of Juan Temple and effected an organization called the "Defenders of Public Safety."[32] A petition was drawn up and signed by fifty-five persons; all were local residents and included such names as William Wolfskill, Juan José Warner, Samuel Prentice, Lemuel Carpenter, Victor Prudon (Prudhomme) and Manuel Arzaga.[33] The petition was an

31 Warner, *Historical Sketch of Los Angeles County,* 25.

32 Charles C. Baker, "The Dispensing of Justice under the Mexican Regime," in *Annual Publications of the Historical Society of Southern California,* x (1913), 38; J. Gregg Layne, "Annals of Los Angeles," in *California Historical Society Quarterly,* xiii (September 1934), 221.

33 Junta Defensora de la Seguridad Pública, April 7, 1836. *Los Angeles Archives,* i, p. 87.

interesting document and was headed by that famous rule in the Roman Twelve Tables *Salus populi supreme lex esto* (Let the welfare of the people be the supreme law). Further, it declared that crime had been increasing rapidly due to the excessive delays in punishment and included the warning that "the blood of the murderers be shed today or ours will be." [34]

The petition was delivered to the alcalde and a special session of the *ayuntamiento* was held on April 7, 1836. The Mexican officials announced that they were unable to grant the request for capital punishment made in the petition, but that justice would be done. Not satisfied, the "Defenders" took matters into their own hands. A body of armed men removed the two accused captives from the prison and took them to the plaza. Gervacio Alipáz and his accomplice were then publicly shot. This action caused the general seizure of firearms which took place at the end of the following month. In the account books of the *ayuntamiento,* Guillermo Wolfskill is credited with "un rifle, $18." [35] The "Defenders of Public Safety" disbanded.

The Wolfskill family lived on the slope of the hill between what are now Spring and New High Streets. One of their neighbors, a local silversmith named Francisco Araujo, spent some of his time visiting Luz Valencia. Apparently he spent more time with

---

[34] Baker, "Dispensing of Justice," 39-40; Warner, *Historical Sketch of Los Angeles County,* 25.

[35] Lista, May 28, 1836. *Los Angeles Archives,* I, p. 100.

her than can be considered appropriate, because some time during 1837, when Francisco Araujo was exiled from California by Carlos Carrillo, Luz Valencia went with him. The pair went to Sinaloa, Mexico, leaving Wolfskill with the two small children, Susana and Timoteo. Araujo was later killed in a duel in Sinaloa, but Luz Valencia did not return to Los Angeles.[36]

On February 14, 1838, a young man from New Mexico rode his tired mule slowly into the center of the pueblo. The weary traveler stopped the first man he saw and inquired the whereabouts of "Billy Wolfskill." [37] The man, who was Juan José Warner, informed the stranger that Wolfskill had made a short trip into the mountains near Los Angeles to set out staves for his wine vats. He asked the newcomer's name. It was John Reid Wolfskill. When it became known that he was Wolfskill's younger brother, John was warmly welcomed by the residents. Don Antonio María Lugo offered to go out into the mountains on horseback and inform Wolfskill of his brother's arrival. William did not recognize his brother when he first saw him because of John's pale and haggard appearance. The younger Wolfskill had suffered a serious illness at Durango, Mexico, and the hardships of the overland journey to California had further obscured his identity. John, of course, knew his older brother immediately and the two were united after

36 Victoriano Vega, "Vida Californiana," MS, p. 18, Bancroft Library.

37 John R. Wolfskill, "A Short Biographical Sketch of the Life and Early Pioneering of J. R. Wolfskill," MS 61, Bancroft Library.

a separation of ten years. The last time the brothers had been together was in Santa Fe in 1828 while William still had a trading business in Taos.[38]

John Wolfskill had spent the intervening years as guard for the transport of treasure between the major cities of Mexico's northern frontier. He passed through Chihuahua, Durango and Matamoros on eleven separate trips out of Santa Fe. In 1833 he returned to Missouri, remained at home for two years, and then re-entered the Santa Fe trade. The year 1836 found John in Sonora, Mexico, a region known for its rich mines, its lucrative trade in horses and mules, and its numerous hostile Indians. John purchased some mules which he planned to sell in New Mexico for enough money to go to California. Unfortunately, Indians attacked his small party and stole all of the mules, but a generous trader by the name of Thompson lent him enough money to make the trip anyway.[39] He left Santa Fe on October 17, 1837 with a party of thirty New Mexicans, one Italian and two Canadians, and reached California after four months' travel. The *ayuntamiento* of Los Angeles, on February 16, 1838, gave permission to this group to "transact business in that part of the province from San Fernando south, but by no means . . . to carry their trade to the north." [40]

John Wolfskill arrived in California during a

[38] Henry D. Barrows, "A Pioneer of Sacramento Valley," in *Annual Publications of the Historical Society of Southern California,* IV (1897), 13.

[39] J. R. Wolfskill, "Biographical Sketch," 2.

[40] Lawrence, "Mexican Trade between Santa Fe and Los Angeles," 31.

period of considerable political strife which at times threatened to cause a civil war between the northern and southern residents of the province. In 1836 a revolution had occurred in the north whereby twenty-seven-year-old Juan Bautista Alvarado was named governor of the "free and sovereign state" of California. The people of Los Angeles and further south had refused to accept this situation. Through the efforts of José Antonio Carrillo, deputy to the national congress in Mexico, southern citizens were able to get Carlos Antonio Carrillo appointed as temporary governor of California in 1838. Alvarado and his partisans in Monterey naturally refused to recognize Carrillo's appointment and the governor sent a sizable force to Los Angeles to arrest those in opposition.

Juan José Warner, quietly conducting business in his plaza store was suddenly confronted by fifteen soldiers demanding that he disclose the hiding place of Pío and Andrés Pico. Warner denied knowing the whereabouts of these supporters of José Antonio Carrillo, but the soldiers accused him of lying and even of hiding the Pico brothers on his premises. They threatened to arrest the shopkeeper and began searching the store. Warner meanwhile picked up a double-barrelled shotgun and challenged the group to carry out the arrest and take him to the guardhouse. The soldiers left for a moment but returned and seized their defiant opponent. In the struggle Warner dropped his gun but continued to fight until his arm was broken. William and John Wolfskill, working near the store, heard the commotion and sprinted to the aid of their friend. William was carrying a rifle and pushed the barrel into the soldiers' faces. About this time Alvarado's men decided to retreat from the scene. Wolfskill heeded Warner's request to not kill any of the assailants and the matter ended with no fatalities.[41] After this the opposition died down and Alvarado managed to retain the governorship of California until 1842.

In March of 1838 William Wolfskill traded his small vineyard for a larger tract of land located on the outskirts of the pueblo approximately within the boundaries of present-day San Pedro and Alameda streets running between Third and Ninth. This land, consisting of about one hundred acres, became the site of Wolfskill's permanent residence and, with the exception of a strip of land fronting on Alameda between Fourth and Sixth streets donated to the Southern Pacific Railroad during the 1870's, remained in the Wolfskill family for the next fifty years. At the time of the exchange, the plot contained several thousand grape vines and a small number of fruit trees.[42] William, with the assistance of his brother John, began making improvements on the land immediately. Rows of newly-set grape vines soon replaced the open fields and between the years 1838

[41] Lorrin L. Morrison, *Warner: The Man and the Ranch* (Los Angeles, 1962), 15-16.

[42] Harris Newmark, *Sixty Years in Southern California* (New York, 1930), 562.

and 1846 Wolfskill planted 32,000 new vines.[43] Subsequently he became one of the leading vineyardists
of the country, having affirmed his belief that "the
plant, if well cared for, would flourish a hundred
years."[44]

Also during the year 1838 work was begun on
Wolfskill's adobe dwelling which today would stand
between Alameda and Central near Fourth street.
Most of the houses throughout Los Angeles were
built with adobe walls three or four feet thick which
served as good insulation against extremes of temperature. The composition was such, however, that
unless protected by overhanging roofs and verandas,
the mud would slowly wash away. The roof itself,
in order to gain protection from the sun, was covered
with asphalt extracted from the nearby La Brea tar
pits. According to family tradition, the Wolfskill
children used some of the "strange looking bones"
found in the pitch as playthings. During the 1850's
a number of the local residents added a second story
to their adobes with an outside staircase, but the
Wolfskill house remained a large, rambling, one-
story rectangular structure with a vine-covered porch
and a spacious courtyard.

Completed in 1839, the Wolfskill residence, called
the "Old Adobe," took its place among the dig-

---

43 "Wolfskill's Vineyard and Orchard at Los Angeles," in San Francisco
Daily Evening Bulletin, Dec. 17, 1858. John Wolfskill was critical of the
haphazard method by which the Indians planted vineyards and cultivated
them with a hoe. Rows were planted in order to enable the use of a plow.

44 Newmark, *Sixty Years in Southern California*, 199.

nified, well-furnished homes of early Los Angeles.[45] Apparently Don Guillermo was becoming accustomed to the finer things, as he ordered a hand-carved, cherry wood four-poster bed and later had a Chickering grand piano shipped to him around Cape Horn. He furnished the home with excellent taste and even imported a silver tea service from England. Unfortunately the Wolfskill adobe was torn down in 1898 to make room for a "magnificent new railroad station" and the remainder of the "Wolfskill Orchard Tract" was subdivided and offered to private sale at that time.[46]

During the latter part of 1838 business was not as profitable or items as easily attainable for all pueblo residents as for Wolfskill. One indication of the climate of business activity is given by a petition signed by nine citizens on November 9, 1838, and directed to the *ayuntamiento*. These owners of small stores in the Plaza area were protesting a new regulation which would prohibit them from selling liquor on Sundays and based their declaration upon the following argument:

> Never before has the circulation of money been so contracted in this city, likewise business depression has never been so great as at the present time, assuring you that in the ordinary week days, scarcely a quart of anything is sold; in view of the above we beg that you allow us to carry on the liquor business on Sundays, from the time that mass is concluded to the hour of the ringing of the bells to pray for the

---

[45] "Wolfskill's Vineyard and Orchard," *loc. cit.*
[46] Newmark, *Sixty Years in Southern California*, 562.

souls in purgatory, as previously established, to see if by this manner we can do a medium business. . .[47]

The new regulation was not enforced and during 1839 business activity picked up as several trading caravans and additional settlers arrived from Santa Fe. The *ayuntamiento* received numerous petitions for tracts of lands, issued licenses for new stores and in general handled the many problems characteristic of a small but growing town.[48]

By 1840 California society had assimilated with little difficulty or incident a number of *yanquis* who had become leading citizens of the community. Several Boston ship captains as well as merchants, traders and ex-mountain men from east of the Rocky Mountains had become naturalized Mexican citizens and married into established Hispanic California families. However, a new era was beginning. In the northern part of the state a Swiss immigrant by the name of John Sutter was building a self-sustaining colony which would play a prominent role in attracting many foreign residents, and in Missouri the Western Emigration Society was organized to send even more. Within a few years the balance which had been maintained between the native *Californios* and their adopted compatriots during the decade of the 1830's would begin to tilt seriously and would eventually be destroyed by the new arrivals.

In 1840 William Wolfskill, former mountain man,

47 Petition to the Ayuntamiento, Nov. 9, 1838. *Los Angeles Archives*, I, p. 609.
48 See *Los Angeles Archives*, I, II and III.

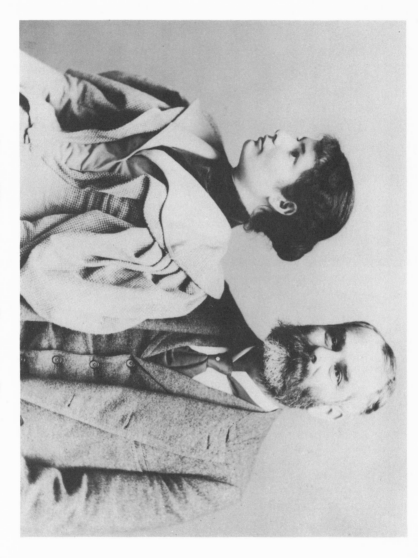

JOSEPH WOLFSKILL AND HIS DAUGHTER, ELENA
Son and granddaughter of William Wolfskill.
Courtesy, Historical Collections, Security First National Bank, Los Angeles.

DINING ROOM OF WILLIAM WOLFSKILL'S "OLD ADOBE"

PARLOR OF THE "OLD ADOBE"
The portrait at center background is a painting of Miguel de Pedrorena.
Both of above photographs courtesy of John C. Wolfskill.

PATIO OF WOLFSKILL'S "OLD ADOBE"

SIDE VIEW OF THE "OLD ADOBE"
Both of the above photographs are reproduced by courtesy of the
Historical Collections, Security First National Bank, Los Angeles.

MR. AND MRS. JOHN C. WOLFSKILL
Courtesy, Historical Collections, Security First National Bank, Los Angeles.

MOVING A WOLFSKILL PALM TREE TO EXPOSITION PARK, LOS ANGELES
Courtesy, Historical Collections, Security First National Bank, Los Angeles.

was one of those well-established *yanquis* in the pueblo of Los Angeles. His adobe home was completed
and his vineyards prospering. His two children,
Susana and Timoteo, were healthy and enjoyed playing in the large garden adjoining the main house.
But life was hardly complete since their mother had
left. Wolfskill spent part of his leisure time visiting
friends on nearby ranchos, and especially enjoyed
seeing his old friend Don Antonio María Lugo. The
Lugo house at Rancho San Antonio was the first
place Wolfskill had stopped upon his arrival in California and he always enjoyed the family's lavish
hospitality. At one of the frequent gatherings held
at the large adobe ranch house, Don Antonio presented Wolfskill to his niece Magdalena, who was
visiting in Los Angeles. They immediately became
good friends.

On Sunday, January 17, 1841, the American brig
"Bolivar" set sail from Santa Barbara bound for the
port of San Pedro. In the cabin sat Don Guillermo
and his bride. Five days before, Wolfskill had married Doña María Magdalena Lugo, daughter of Don
José Ygnacio Lugo and Doña Rafaela Romero de
Lugo of Santa Barbara.[49] Magdalena's family numbered among the oldest and most prominent of the
Spanish California residents. Her father, José Ygnacio, the son of Francisco Salvador de Lugo, was
the second native child of Spanish extraction to be
born in California and was confirmed by Father

---

[49] Francis Mellus, "Journal of Voyages to, from, and along the Coast of
California," MS 29, Huntington Library.

Junípero Serra at Mission San Antonio de Padua in 1778.[50] Her uncle, Antonio María Lugo, received one of the few land grants made during the Spanish period. Granted in 1810, Rancho San Antonio consisted of about thirty thousand acres adjoining the pueblo of Los Angeles to the southeast. Among her father's sisters were María Antonia Lugo de Vallejo, mother of Mariano Guadalupe Vallejo,[51] and the wives of Pablo Antonio Cota, José Raimundo Carrillo and José Pedro Ruiz.[52] Within the Lugo family group were some of the most elegant of the Plaza homes and spacious ranch houses. Magdalena's mother, Doña Rafaela Romero, was born at the royal presidio of Loreto in Baja California in 1779, and accompanied her parents to the presidio of Santa Barbara in 1781. Doña Rafaela married Don José Ygnacio Lugo on June 13, 1800 in the mission church of Santa Barbara. The couple's second child, María Magdalena, was born at the nearby presidio on May 11, 1804.[53]

Magdalena Lugo de Wolfskill spent the majority

50 Thomas W. Temple, "Wolfskill Genealogy," MS in the possession of John C. Wolfskill, Los Angeles, California.

51 Commander in chief of the military forces in California during much of the Mexican period, Vallejo was the owner of extensive land holdings in the Sonoma Valley, uncle of Governor Juan Bautista Alvarado (1836-1842), and a strong supporter of Americans in California.

52 José del Carmen Lugo, "Vida de un Ranchero," as told to Thomas Savage, 1877, and translated by Helen Pruitt Beattie in the *San Bernardino County Museum Association Quarterly,* VIII (Winter 1961), p. 1.

53 Certificate of Baptism, May 13, 1804. Iglesia de Nuestra Señora de los Dolores, Santa Barbara, California. God-parents were Carlos Carrillo and María Antonia Carrillo.

of her childhood at Santa Barbara. As a young lady, she devoted generously of her time to the Franciscan fathers at the mission and assisted in their teaching of the Indians. Wolfskill always kept the proceeds from four orange trees in front of the "Old Adobe" and donated them to the fathers at Santa Barbara each year in memory of his wife's interest in Indian education. After their marriage, the Wolfskills made frequent visits to the Santa Barbara area.

The first child of William and Magdalena Wolfskill was a daughter, Juana Josefa, born in Los Angeles on November 23, 1841. In the years following, the Wolfskills became the parents of María Francisca, José Guillermo, María Magdalena and Luis María.[54] All of these children grew up at the Wolfskill ranch in Los Angeles and later remained in California to become permanent and influential members of the community. One more child, María Rafaela, was born in 1851 but died of illness at the age of four.[55]

All of Wolfskill's daughters made successful marriages. In 1853 Susana married Henry C. Cardwell, an American who had come to California just before the Mexican War. Cardwell worked for Wolfskill on his ranch and experimented with a number of new plants, especially strawberries, which he succeeded in growing by 1856. The Cardwells had three chil-

[54] Libro primero de Bautismos, 216, 238, 240, 307, 368. Iglesia de Nuestra Señora de Los Angeles.

[55] Henry D. Barrows, "Diary," Jan. 18, 1855. In private collection of Mrs. Thomas P. Cullen.

dren, William, Leonora and Charles. Henry Cardwell constructed a new house for his family on land
adjoining the Wolfskill property in 1858, but in 1859
tragedy struck. In February son Charles died of illness and in July of the same year Henry also died.[56]
Susana returned to the Wolfskill home until July of
1860, when she married Elijah T. Moulton.[57] Moulton was a Canadian who had joined an expedition to
California in 1844 and served in Fremont's forces
during the Mexican campaign. In 1850 he was made
a deputy sheriff in Los Angeles and also worked for
one of Wolfskill's neighbors. By 1855 Moulton had
purchased some land near the "Old Adobe" and became a good friend of the Wolfskill family. Shortly
afterwards he was placed in charge of a portion of
the Wolfskill property. After Cardwell's death,
Moulton retained Susana's friendship and married
her a year later. The couple acquired one hundred
fifty acres in East Los Angeles and were among the
earliest settlers of that region. Unfortunately, tragedy
came again and Susana Wolfskill died in 1861.[58]

Juana Josefa married Henry D. Barrows, a Connecticut school teacher who arrived in California in
1852. Barrows lived at the Wolfskill home from 1854
until his marriage to Juana in 1860. They became the
parents of one daughter, Alice, before Juana's sad

---

56 Los Angeles *Star,* July 16, 1859.

57 Libro Tercero de Matrimonios Perteneciente a esta Misión de San
Gabriel, Libro Primero de Los Angeles, Acta 577, p. 60.   Iglesia de Nuestra Señora de Los Angeles.

58 Newmark, *Sixty Years in Southern California,* 171.

and premature death in 1863. María Francisca married a native of Los Angeles, Charles J. Shephard. Shephard was one of the early fruit packers and shippers of the city and dealt in all kinds of general produce. He owned a packing house on the corner of Main and Jefferson Streets and worked with his brothers-in-law José and Luis Wolfskill in the distribution of the Wolfskill oranges, lemons and other fruits. The youngest daughter, Magdalena, married another native of Los Angeles, Francisco Sabichi. The son of Mateo and Josefa Franco Sabichi,[59] Francisco was educated in Europe, commissioned a petty officer in the English Navy and then returned to California in the 1860's. After his marriage to Magdalena Wolfskill in 1865, Francisco remained in Los Angeles as a prominent citizen and served five terms on the city council. The Sabichis resided on a twenty acre tract at Seventh and San Pedro Streets and reared a family of eleven children.[60]

José Guillermo, the eldest son of William and Magdalena Wolfskill, was born in 1844. From his earliest childhood, José was interested in the plants and trees of his father's ranch and in later life pursued a successful career in agriculture. Not only did he maintain the property between Alameda and San Pedro Streets, but acquired a nursery in Brooklyn Heights and a florist shop on Fourth Street. During

[59] Sister of Antonio Franco Coronel.

[60] John Steven McGroarty, *California of the South* (Chicago, 1935), v, p. 349. The children were Agatha, Joseph, George, William, Louis, Beatrice, Francis, Mary, Johanna, Leopold and Rose.

the 1860's Joseph Wolfskill, as he became known in
the American period, served two terms on the Los
Angeles city council and on both the land and water
commissions. In 1869 he married Doña Elena de
Pedrorena, the youngest daughter of Don Miguel de
Pedrorena [61] and Doña María Antonia Estudillo de
Pedrorena of San Diego.[62] Elena shared in the in-
heritance of El Cajon Rancho in 1876 and received
about 12,000 acres of land comprising Rancho San
Jacinto upon the death of her father in 1889.[63] The
latter rancho, located in Riverside County, was primarily used for stock raising. Joseph and Elena remained at the Wolfskill residence, the "Old Adobe,"
and reared a family of twelve children. Those who
grew up on the original orchard site included Fede-
rico, José Ignacio, Inocenta, Elena, Ruth, David,
John Christian, Grace, Luis and Martin. Two of the
children died before reaching maturity. The Wolfskills moved to a "handsome residence" in Redondo
Beach in 1887, remained there until 1898, and then
returned to live permanently in Los Angeles.[64]

---

61 Miguel de Pedrorena was one of the few delegates to the California
Constitutional Convention of 1849 who was born in Spain (Madrid). He
had been in California for twelve years as a shipping agent, favored the
intervention of the United States and was made Stockton's aide and col-
lector of customs at San Diego. See Donald E. Hargis, "Native Californians in the Constitutional Convention of 1849," in *California Historical
Society Quarterly,* XXXVI (March 1954), 3-13.

62 María Antonia Estudillo was the daughter of San Diego landholder
and government official José Antonio Estudillo. See Bancroft, *History of
California,* II, p. 793.

63 José Antonio Estudillo was the original grantee of Rancho San Jacinto
in 1842.

64 McGroarty, *California of the South,* V, pp. 188-92.

Luis María Wolfskill, William's youngest son, also inherited his father's interest in agriculture. Luis was educated at a military school in San Francisco but returned to Los Angeles upon completion of his studies. He later married Luisa Dalton whose father, Londoner Henry Dalton, was the owner of Rancho Santa Anita during the 1850's.[65] Luis Wolfskill eventually acquired both Rancho Azusa de Duarte and Rancho Santa Anita and became an influential citizen of the community. He served two terms on the Los Angeles city council. Luis and Luisa became the parents of seven children before Luis's premature death in 1884 at the age of thirty-six.[66]

[65] *Ibid.,* 235.

[66] The children were William, Alice, Frank, Isabel, Herbert, Julian and one who died in infancy.

5

The Sacramento Valley

The flashing and golden pageant of California,
The sudden and gorgeous drama,
*   the sunny and ample lands . . .*
And wool and wheat and the grape,
*   and diggings of yellow gold.*
*   – Walt Whitman*

By 1840 the Wolfskill ranch in Los Angeles had become a center of agricultural activity, but John Wolfskill was not exactly satisfied to devote all of his time to his brother's ever-expanding fields. Being an ardent agriculturist himself, he was eager to experiment with other varieties of plants and in new methods of cultivation. It was his great ambition to have a ranch of his own, but the majority of good land in southern California had already been granted to a Lugo, a Domínguez, a Verdugo or one of the other early Spanish families. Much of the fertile land with easy access to water had been granted as early as 1784, and many other choice sections had been assigned to retiring soldiers after the secularization of the missions. Because John Wolfskill had no means by which he could purchase a rancho, he had to look for some other way.

Juan José Warner, who had traversed just about all of California's Central Valley with Ewing Young, told John that there was good land still available in

northern California. Warner recalled that after a
"month's experience of amphibious life" in the spring
of 1833, he "had wallowed out of the flooded lands
of the Sacramento Valley and reached the dry land
near the banks of the Putah Creek." [1] He noticed the
vast stretch of fertile land which lay between the
Coast ranges and the marshes of the Sacramento and
thought it to be ideally suited for agriculture. Putah
Creek, which today marks the dividing line between
Yolo and Solano Counties, could be used for irrigation as it cut its way across the land.

Armed with at least some knowledge of the land,
John Wolfskill rode northward in 1840. Continuing
beyond San Francisco Bay, he finally reached Sonoma and called upon Don Mariano Guadalupe
Vallejo, military comandante of the northern district
of California. Vallejo was at that time administering
the numerous livestock of the now secularized mission of San Francisco de Solano, and commanding
his somewhat ragged troops. Vallejo ruled his district
with a firm hand and it was necessary to obtain his
approval before anyone could obtain land north of
the bay. When John made known his purposes, the
general told him to look over the country as much as
he liked, but that he would not recommend any grant
of land. The statement was final. John Wolfskill was
not a citizen of Mexico, and it was probably for that
reason that Vallejo withheld his approval. John, fail-

---

1 Warner, "Reminiscences of Early California," 187.

ing to complete his objective, returned to his brother's home in Los Angeles.[2]

In the following year, 1841, John decided to make one more attempt to obtain the land from General Vallejo. Also by this time William had become interested in cattle raising and was looking for more land himself. Promising to give John whatever support which might be necessary in order to obtain a land grant, William sent his younger brother again to Sonoma to make the final plea to Vallejo. Before seeing the general, John decided to make a final decision on the location of his grant, should he be fortunate enough to receive one. He explored the country to the north of San Francisco Bay and from all of the unoccupied land in that region, he selected four square leagues [3] on Putah Creek. The site which Warner had mentioned was apparently best suited to his purposes. The creek, which was also known as Río de los Putos, seemed to flow out of a gap in the Coast Range, run south for a short distance, and then turn east, finally disappearing in the Sacramento swamps. For the first mile after leaving the canyon, it ran through gently rolling hills amidst great spreading oaks, but then the character of the countryside effected a marked change in its pattern. "Dipping gently to the east there streched away a fertile,

---

[2] Barrows, "A Pioneer of Sacramento Valley," 13-14.

[3] A square league contains 4,428.402 acres. William Carey Jones in *Land Titles in California* (Washington, 1850) refers to a league square "as the smallest measurement of rural property spoken of."

even prairie, then covered with a luxurious growth of wild oats." [4]

John again approached Vallejo at Sonoma, but this time by sending in his place, one Mark West, an Englishman and resident of Sonoma. But the answer was still the same and "Mr. Wolfskill made up his mind to abandon further attempts to obtain land there or anywhere in California and to return south to leave the territory." [5]

However, as he was about to leave, John Wolfskill was hailed by Jacob P. Leese, son-in-law of Mariano Vallejo. Leese had arrived in California in 1833 and had carried on a merchandise business in Los Angeles for several years before moving north to Yerba Buena (San Francisco). When Leese learned that William Wolfskill's brother was seeking land in northern California, he offered to help. He told John to contact him again and in the meantime he would see what could be done. Leese succeeded in overcoming the comandante's objections and obtained his approval for a grant of four square leagues or 17,754.73 acres,[6] of public domain lying on both sides of Putah Creek. This was done, however, with the understanding that it would be made in the name of William Wolfskill, a citizen of

---

[4] Extracts from the field notes of Henry Hancock, Deputy U.S. Surveyor, "Transcript of Record." U.S. District Court Records, Northern District of California, *The United States vs. William Wolfskill*, Case no. 232, pp. 117-18.

[5] Barrows, "A Pioneer of Sacramento Valley," 14.

[6] Ogden G. Hoffman, *District Judge Reports of Land Cases* (San Francisco, 1862), I, appendix 32.

Mexico. At last successful, John returned to Los Angeles.[7]

On February 6, 1842, Jacob P. Leese, at Sonoma, drew up and signed for William Wolfskill a petition to the comandante general, formally requesting his recommendation for the grant. This petition, or *expediente,* read as follows:

> I, WILLIAM WOLFSKILL, a resident of this National Department of Upper California, before Your Honor respectfully show that possessing a certain quantity of major and minor livestock not having any place wherein to put them unless Your Honor may please to grant to me a tract of land in fee upon which I may collect them, and which I ask Your Honor to locate on a tract called Rio de los Putos situated on the north of this frontier; and if it may please Your Honor to grant to me the aforesaid land I ask that it may consist of four square leagues (sitios de ganado mayor) so that I may locate my stock, and as soon as it may please Your Honor to grant me the said land you may request the Departmental Government to provide in justice for all the necessary requirements in order to obtain the grant in fee of the land I petition for. Please admit this petition on Common paper as there is none in the place of corresponding stamp.
>
> I swear what may be necessary, Sonoma, Feby 6th, 1842.
>
> J. P. LEESE
> for William Wolfskill [8]

William evidently visited the rancho site some time in 1841 because Juan Warner, who was then living at the Wolfskill home, drew a map of the grant in 1841 from directions "given by William Wolfskill,

[7] Barrows, "Pioneer of Sacramento Valley," 14.
[8] Expediente, *U.S. vs. Wolfskill, op. cit.,* 64.

who had been on the land a short time before." [9] The
two men prepared all of the papers, including the
diseño or map, which were necessary for soliciting a
land grant from the governor of California, and
began to speculate upon the possibilities of the new
ranch. It was now the spring of 1842 and because
Warner had some business in Monterey, he agreed
to take the papers to Governor Juan Bautista de
Alvarado, nephew of Mariano Vallejo. Wolfskill
assumed Alvarado would make the grant without
delay. The matter was not, however, as simple as it
seemed, because certain formalities were lacking in
Vallejo's recommendation to the governor, and Alvarado refused to consider the application until the
defects were remedied.[10] Warner could not wait for
the corrections to be made and had to return to Los
Angeles. But Thomas O. Larkin, who at this time
was the foremost merchant in Monterey, took the
papers to Sonoma and had them put in the proper
form. When he returned to Monterey, Larkin
brought the papers with him and held them until
the arrival of John Wolfskill in May of 1842.[11]

Again in Los Angeles, Warner acting as William's
attorney, drew up the final *expediente* for the grant.
This was forwarded by ship to Larkin at Monterey.
In the letter which accompanied the *expediente*

9 Deposition of Juan José Warner, *ibid.*, 42.

10 Barrows, "Pioneer of Sacramento Valley," 15.

11 Mellus, "Journal of Voyages to, from and along the Coast of California," (Huntington Library, MS), states that Larkin was in San Francisco
on April 30, 1842. It is probable that he secured the decree at this time.

Warner asked Larkin to present the petition to the
governor and procure the title to the grant.[12] However, it was through John Wolfskill that the final
petition was finally presented to Alvarado.

In the early part of May, 1842, at about the same
time the petition was sent, John set out on horseback
to the capital, driving a herd of cattle and horses
before him. When he arrived in Monterey, he obtained all of the papers from Larkin and prepared
to take them to the governor. Probably recalling his
first encounter with Vallejo, he decided not to take
any chances with diplomacy. Hiring George Allen,
a versatile Irishman who had resided in California
since 1822, John had this "competent interpreter"
present the petition, the map, his brother's naturalization papers and other documents to the governor,
who, without further delay, signed the grant on May
24, 1842.[13]

In this final grant, Alvarado declared that:

Whereas, William Wolfskill, a naturalized Mexican, for
his benefit and that of his family, has made application for a
tract of land bounded on the East by the Bullrush Swamp
and on the west by the hills and located on the banks of the
River called Los Putos, having previously taken the legal
steps and made the proper investigations agreeable to the provisions of the laws and regulations, by virtue of the powers
conferred upon me in the name of the Mexican Nation, I
have granted him the above mentioned land declaring him

[12] J. J. Warner to Thomas O. Larkin, May 2, 1842. Larkin Documents, I, no. 268, Bancroft Library.
[13] Barrows, "Pioneer of Sacramento Valley," 15.

the owner of it by these present letters, subject to the approbation of the Most Excellent Departmental Junta and subject to the following conditions: [14]

William Wolfskill could "fence his land without injury to the crossings, roads and servitudes," and could "freely and exclusively enjoy the same" and "direct it to such use and cultivation as he saw fit, but within one year he was to erect a house and have it inhabited." Also he was to "apply to the respective judge in order that he be given judicial possession by virtue of this title." The judge was to mark the boundaries of the grant and Wolfskill was to plant some fruit or forest trees at their limits. The grant was for four square leagues as shown by the map which accompanied the *expediente* and any land over that was to remain with the Mexican government. Furthermore, it was stated that if Wolfskill "should contravene these conditions, he will lose his right to the land and it will be subject to denouncement by any other person." [15]

William Wolfskill had intended to name his rancho Lihuaytos, after the Indian *rancheria* which was once located on the land. By the time he learned the name, however, it had been appropriated by Manuel Vaca, the owner of a neighboring rancho. Thus Wolfskill's rancho became known as Río de los Putos.[16]

Upon the conclusion of his business in Monterey,

14 Final Grant to William Wolfskill, *U.S. vs. Wolfskill*, 61-62.

15 *Ibid.*, 62-63.

16 Helen D. Crystal, *The Beginnings of Vacaville, California* (Unpublished MA thesis, University of California, 1923), 124-25.

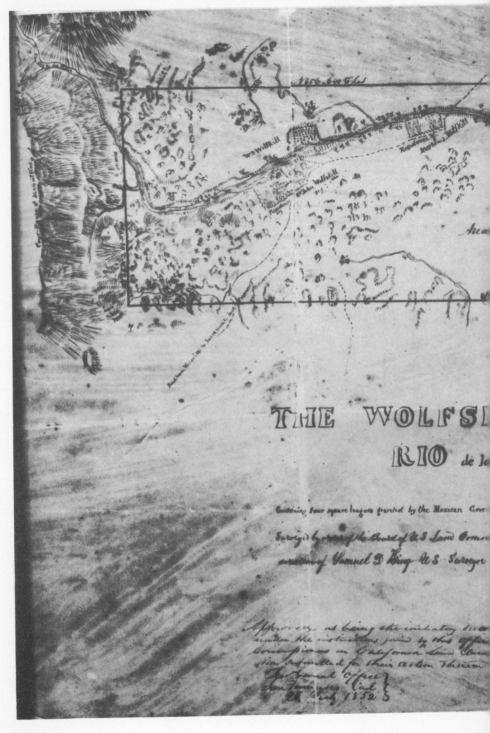

...3551, 419 Square Chains
— 17385 $\frac{1000}{10000}$ Acres

7656 28 Chas

Wolfskill &
J. McMahon

ILL RANCHO
PUTOS

...nt to Guillermo Wolfskill   May AD 1842

...m for California date May 15. 1852 and under the

...al for California during the month of June AD 1852

By Henry Hancock Deputy

...d the claim mentioned specified
...ny int... effect the orders of the
...in ... on the 15. May 1852 ...

James King
Surveyor Genl
BANCROFT
LIBRARY

John set out for the new rancho. It had been agreed
that although William owned the land, John would
live on it and take care of his brother's cattle. Herd-
ing before him his twenty-four mares, ten tame
horses, three yoke of oxen, several milk cows and a
number of other cattle, John Wolfskill moved along
until he reached the San Joaquin. He found the river
flooded and was forced to cross back over the hills to
San Jose and then proceed up the west side of the
bay to Yerba Buena, as San Francisco was then
called.

Leaving his cattle near Mission Dolores in charge
of a young Mexican, John continued on to the ranch
of George C. Yount in the Napa Valley. Yount had
done well since his otter hunting days and had become a successful rancher. In 1835 he had begun to
work for Mariano Vallejo at Sonoma and had greatly
impressed the General by making shingles for various
buildings in the area. Vallejo decided that such industry should be rewarded, so in 1836 he offered
Yount a grant of four square leagues in the Napa
Valley. Yount declined the generous offer stating
that because he did not have the means or the livestock to handle such a large amount, he would much
prefer just one half league. Vallejo, however, insisted
that the Mexican government could not possibly
grant such a small area – a mere 2,214 acres, and that
he would have to take more. After a unique discus-
sion, the two men compromised on two square
leagues. Yount built a flour mill, later a sawmill,
and cultivated the land. In 1841 he received news of

his family and in 1843 was joined by two of his daughters who had come overland with the Chiles expedition. The ex-fur trapper always maintained good relations with the neighboring Indians and other residents of the valley, although in later years he had some trouble with squatters. The portion of his holdings which he managed to save is now the site of present-day Yountville. George C. Yount died in his Napa Valley home in 1865 at the age of 71.[17]

John Wolfskill remained with Yount during the summer of 1842 and was employed on the ranch off and on until the next fall. Apparently John had brought his horses to Yount's ranch because he set out from there in July of 1842 with a band of them for Río de los Putos.[18] Crossing the mountains east of Napa, he passed through Green Valley to Suisun Valley and then traveled northward through the present site of Vacaville to his rancho.[19]

When John arrived, he found the place completely deserted except for the wild animals. In fact the lonely aspect of the place so affected him that according to testimony "direct from the lips of John R. Wolfskill himself," he passed the first night on his new domain high up in the fork of a tree "away from the possible hug of prowling grizzlies and the presence of creeping things."[20]

[17] Bancroft, *History of California,* v, p. 783; U.S. District Court Records, Northern District of California, *The United States vs. George C. Yount,* Case no. 32.

[18] Deposition of John R. Wolfskill, *U.S. vs. Wolfskill,* 34.

[19] Gregory, *History of Solano and Napa Counties,* 58.

[20] *Ibid.,* 59.

John's first concern was to build a house, which he did out of tule, willow brush and mud. This structure, which he necessarily rebuilt periodically, remained his home until after the boom days of the gold rush.[21] Late in the fall, when the rivers were low, he returned to Mission Dolores for his cattle, which he drove home by way of San Jose and Livermore. He swam them across the San Joaquin at a place called "El Pescadero" and crossed the Sacramento River at Sutter's Fort.[22] At about this time William's agent, William D. M. Howard of Los Angeles and San Francisco, bought more cattle in San Jose. These arrived at the ranch some time towards the end of 1842 or in the early part of 1843.[23]

Except for taking care of the stock, no work was done on the ranch during the winter of 1842-43, but in the spring ground-breaking was begun. Two immigrants, Samuel Green McMahan and "Doctor" William Wiggins, had sought shelter at Río de los Putos and for a time John employed them on the land.[24] With their help, John set out a number of fruit trees, and as early as January, 1843, he commenced sowing barley. In April, corn and beans were planted and before summer arrived a small vineyard of mission grapes had been set out.[25]

The stock was allowed to range at will along both

---

[21] Deposition of John R. Wolfskill, *U.S. vs. Wolfskill*, 34.

[22] Barrows, "Pioneer of Sacramento Valley," 15.

[23] Deposition of J. J. Warner, *U.S. vs. Wolfskill*, 13.

[24] Ellen Lamont Wood, "Samuel Green McMahan," in *California Historical Society Quarterly*, XXIII (December 1944), 289.

[25] Deposition of John R. Wolfskill, *U.S. vs. Wolfskill*, 34-35.

sides of Putah Creek as far as five or six miles below the house and two or three miles above it.[26] Constant vigil was necessary to guard against thieving Indians or roaming Mexicans; but the greatest danger was from fire. The dry wild oats, if once ignited, burned with fearful rapidity.[27]

John Bidwell, the famous overland pioneer who led a party from Missouri to California in 1841, visited Río de los Putos in March of 1843. He found that the ranch had a corral and two dwelling places. The next year he returned for another visit and found that the cultivated area had been extended to the opposite side of the creek, where additional corrals and several houses of adobe and wood had been constructed. Forty acres were cleared and bearing flourishing crops of corn, wheat and barley. There was also a vineyard and an orchard of various fruit trees.[28]

In June of 1844 the Wolfskills were unfairly dispossessed of their land by Manuel Vaca through an order of Governor Manuel Micheltorena.[29] In 1842 Vaca and Juan Felipe Peña had come from New Mexico to California and settled on Putah Creek. They obtained a grant of ten leagues and the land was referred to as the Lihuaytos, the Indian name of the creek. The ten leagues covered much of the country near the present towns of Davis, Tremont,

---

[26] Deposition of John Bidwell, *ibid.*, 23.

[27] Gregory, *History of Solano and Napa Counties*, 58.

[28] Deposition of John Bidwell, *U.S. vs. Wolfskill*, 22-23.

[29] Deposition of J. J. Warner, *ibid.*, 35.

Dixon, and Batavia, and bordered the Wolfskill ranch. According to a document written by Judge John Curry, former chief justice of the Supreme Court who died in Dixon at the age of 98, "this tract of land was a waste, barren of trees for the most part, while that of Wolfskill, being the older grant, was beautifully adorned with oaks, affording shelter for men and cattle. Vaca and Peña coveted the valley covered by the Wolfskill grant, and by force drove John Wolfskill from it." [30] Vaca then claimed that Wolfskill's grant was for land that was a portion of a grant made to him. Through a series of some obviously underhanded legal dealings, Vaca succeeded in getting an order signed by Micheltorena which forced John Wolfskill to leave his home and take up residence with a neighbor. The matter was taken to the court in the Northern District but no settlement was reached as the judge required the personal appearance of William, who was then unable to make the trip from Los Angeles.

After much delay, the affair was finally thrashed out before the Primary Court of Claims in Los Angeles. In July, 1845, a temporary agreement was reached by which Vaca was to withdraw from Río de los Putos. In the following November, however, the two were battling again in court. This time a final settlement was made. It was agreed on November 17, 1845, that William Wolfskill should have his four

[30] Wyman Riley, "Sunday Notebook," in Vallejo News-Chronicle, Dec. 19, 1958.

square leagues measured, and that if after measurement, the land along the river bank below his rancho
was so small that Vaca could not use it, William was
to purchase said land.[31]

The next day, Governor Pío Pico, who had by this
time replaced Manuel Micheltorena, ordered Wolfskill to apply to the judge in Sonoma and be put in
possession of the land.[32] In the spring of 1846, in the
company of William D. M. Howard, Wolfskill left
for the north to take care of the situation. On July 7,
1846, a few days before they reached Sonoma, the
Americans "hoisted the flag at Monterey" and there
was no way to complete any judicial transactions.[33]
With the troubles incident to the American occupation, the whole province was thrown into turmoil and
Wolfskill was never able to get legal possession of his
lands or to have the grant measured during the Mexican regime.[34] Besides, the documents pertaining to
the ownership of the rancho were in the hands of
John Wolfskill who had joined Frémont's forces in
the north, and this made it impossible for the grant
to be approved by the departmental deputation during Pico's term in office.[35] The Wolfskills had, however, regained the actual possession and use of the
land.

Late in 1846 Samuel Green McMahan, the mem-

31 *U.S. vs. Wolfskill,* 91-100.
32 *Ibid.,* 78.
33 Gertrude Howard Whitwell, "William Davis Merry Howard," in *California Historical Society Quarterly,* XXVII (June 1948), 108.
34 Petition of William Wolfskill, *U.S. vs. Wolfskill,* 6.
35 Deposition of J. J. Warner, *ibid.,* 12.

ber of the Bidwell expedition of 1841 who had worked for John Wolfskill, returned to the valley to purchase one hundred sixty acres of land on Putah Creek. McMahan had, during the intervening years, helped organize and lead with James Clyman another expedition to California. He now decided to remain and John Wolfskill was pleased to make the sale. At this time Wolfskill considered his nearest neighbors to be John Sutter on the Sacramento River, John Marsh near Mt. Diablo, George Yount in the Napa Valley and Chief Solano's Indians in the Suisun Valley; McMahan was a welcome resident. In 1859 McMahan purchased an adjoining tract of slightly more than 1366 acres from John Wolfskill for $10,933.[36]

In spite of the legal tangle surrounding its title, William and John Wolfskill decided to divide the rancho. By a deed dated August 27, 1849, John was given the portion lying south of Putah Creek.[37] Three years later, on May 14, 1852, William presented the grant for confirmation before the "Board of Commissioners Appointed to Ascertain and Settle Private Land Claims in the State of California" and a survey was ordered.[38] After numerous testimonies and lengthy proceedings carried out in San Francisco during 1853-54, William Wolfskill's original grant to Rancho Río de los Putos was finally confirmed by

---

[36] Wood, "Samuel Green McMahan," 295.

[37] Deed of William Wolfskill to John R. Wolfskill, Aug. 27, 1849, in possession of Mrs. Robert Dart, grand-daughter of John R. Wolfskill, now residing in Sacramento, California.

[38] Petition of William Wolfskill, *U.S. vs. Wolfskill,* 5-6.

the United States Land Commission on November 7, 1854.[39]

After the discovery of gold in California, three other brothers of William and John Reid Wolfskill made their way to the Sacramento Valley. Mathus Wolfskill (1810-1876) had married neighbor Pamela Ashcraft of Howard County, Missouri, and arrived with his family at Putah Creek on September 30, 1850. The Mathus Wolfskills resided there until 1866, when they moved to Suisun Township.[40] Their eldest son John W. attended school at the Collegiate Institute in Benicia until 1854, when he traveled to Los Angeles to live with his Uncle William. John became interested in stock-raising while in the southern part of the state, but returned to Solano County in 1856. His younger brother, Joseph C., then went to live with the William Wolfskills at the "Old Adobe" and remained there until 1860. Several years later, the sons of Mathus Wolfskill decided to invest in a rancho in San Diego County called Rincón del Diablo. The rancho, which consisted of 12,633 acres of land stocked with six hundred horses and mules, was located in *el Valle Escondido* or "Hidden Valley." The Wolfskills purchased the rancho from Judge O. S. Witherbee of San Diego in 1868 for $8,000. The area, which surrounded the present-day town of Escondido, became known as Wolfskill Plains. John lived on Rancho Rincón del Diablo for sixteen years raising cattle and sheep with the assist-

[39] *Ibid.,* 113-15, 119.
[40] Bancroft, *History of California,* v, p. 779.

Samuel K. Holman,

TO

John Wolfskill

Deed.

Dated February 23rd 1884

Consideration, $40,000.00

Granting Clause, Does grant, bargain & sell, convey & confirm.

Estate Granted, all that certain lot &, of land _____

_____ the real property hereinafter described.

Description. Situate in the _____ County of Los

Angeles, State of California, bounded and described as follows, to-wit:

The Rancho known and called the Rancho San Jose de Buenos Ayres granted to Maximo Alanis by Manuel Micheltorena Governor of the Department of the Californias, by grant of date February 4th 1843. and confirmed to Benjamin D. Wilson, and William T. B. Sanford by the District Court of the United States for the Southern District of California on the 18th day of February 1857. bounded in said grant as follows. being to the extent of one square league within said boundaries— On the South by the Rancho of the Machados. on the North by the Sierra. on the West by the Rancho formerly owned by Francisco Sepulveda now deceased; and on the East by land now or formerly belonging to or claimed by Ricardo Vejar, and being the same lands described in the Patent from the Government of the United States to the said Benjamin D. Wilson and William T. B. Sanford. dated July 25th 1866. recorded in Book 3, of Patents page 591. et seq. in the office of the County Recorder of said County of Los Angeles, and to which patent, and the record thereof. reference for a more particular description is hereby made.

DEED TO THE RANCHO SAN JOSE DE BUENOS AYRES

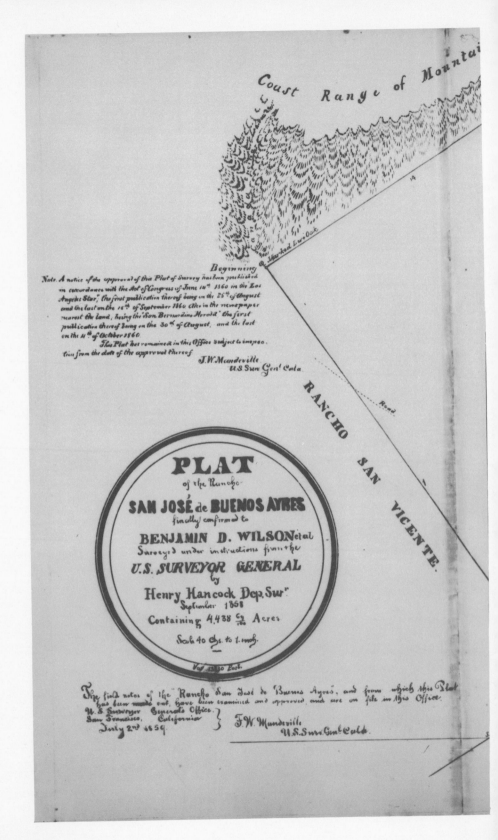

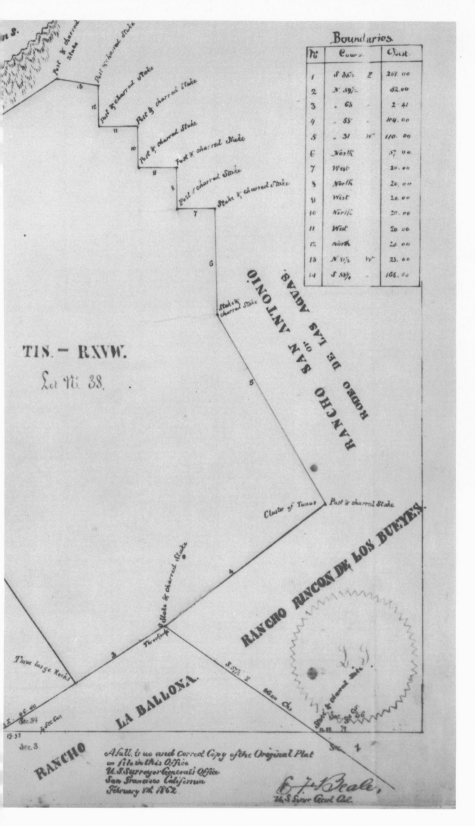

Boundaries

№	Course	Dist.
1	S 35½ E	208.00
2	N 59½	52.00
3	" 63	2.41
4	" 55	104.00
5	" 31 W	110.00
6	North	57.00
7	West	20.00
8	North	20.00
9	West	20.00
10	North	20.00
11	West	20.00
12	North	20.00
13	N 1½ W	23.00
14	S 88½	168.00

RANCHO SAN ANTONIO or RODEO DE LAS AGUAS

TIS. – RXVW.

Lot № 38.

RANCHO RINCON DE LOS BUEYES.

Cluster of Tunas   Post & charred Stake

Three large Rocks

LA BALLONA.

RANCHO

A full, true and correct Copy of the Original Plat
on file in this Office
U.S. Surveyor Generals Office
San Francisco California
February 8th 1862.

E. F. Beale,
U.S. Surr Genl Cal.

ance of some San Pascual Indians whom he had befriended and aided. During this time John served a term as state senator from San Diego and San Bernardino Counties. The Wolfskills sold the rancho in October of 1883 for $128,000 [41] and in turn John bought Rancho San José de Buenos Ayres on the site of present-day Westwood. He paid $40,000 or about $10.00 an acre.[42] Later John sold numerous parcels of land to individual farmers, but retained the majority of the land intact for cultivation. This nephew of William Wolfskill is credited with having introduced large-scale lima bean culture into Los Angeles. John W. Wolfskill lived on Rancho San José until the ranch house was destroyed by fire in 1910.[43] His younger brother Joseph had remained in Suisun.[44]

Sarchel C. Wolfskill (1818-1878) had married another Howard County neighbor, Margaret Ann Cooper, and remained at home in Missouri until the outbreak of the Mexican War. He then enlisted as a private soldier under General Doniphan and served in various campaigns until peace was declared. The discovery of gold in California encouraged him to come west. In 1852 he and his family started for the Pacific Coast via Nicaragua. Mrs. Wolfskill was forced to ride an old mule and carry an infant from Lake Nicaragua to the Pacific Ocean. One of their

[41] Henry D. Barrows, "John Wolfskill," *Annual Report of the Los Angeles County Pioneers of Southern California*, VIII (1913-14), 13.

[42] Deed of Samuel K. Holman to John Wolfskill, Feb. 23, 1884. *Book of Deeds*, no. 119, p. 219, Los Angeles County, California.

[43] Ralph Hancock, *Fabulous Boulevard* (New York, 1949), 184.

[44] Barrows, "John Wolfskill," 13.

children, Milton, died at the Isthmus. After a difficult sea voyage to San Francisco, the Sarchel Wolfskills set out for Solano County to join their brother. They arrived on June 1, 1852, and John Reid Wolfskill gave them a gift of 1200 acres of land. Sarchel remained on this land until his death in 1878. He and his wife Margaret were the parents of twelve children – Milton, Stephen, Elizabeth, Joseph, John, William, Barnett, Mattie, Sallie, Mollie, Nellie and Ruth.[45]

The third and youngest brother to arrive was Milton Wolfskill (1819-1906). Milton had stayed in Howard County until 1848, when he made the long trek across the plains with a mule team to California. He started from Arrow Rock, Missouri, and followed the Oregon – California trail with a large party of settlers and gold seekers. Milton settled on Putah Creek and purchased a large tract of land in order to plant vineyards, orchards, and a sizable quantity of grain. In 1873 this fifth Wolfskill brother and his wife Anna (Sweany), whom he had married in Solano County in 1860,[46] moved to Texas. There they planted a vineyard and cultivated grapes on a large scale, but the venture proved to be unsuccessful. The Wolfskills turned to the raising of grain until 1885, when they sold the ranch and decided to live in Los Angeles. For a time Milton worked with his

---

45 "A sketch of the active part taken in the historical development of California by John R. Wolfskill, Sarchel Wolfskill and William Wolfskill," typescript with notes in the handwriting of David R. Sessions, Bancroft Library.

46 Bancroft, *History of California,* v, p. 779.

nephew, William's son Joseph, in the vineyards and orchards of the "Old Adobe." Milton later became a flagman for the Southern Pacific Railroad, a job which he held until his death in 1906.[47]

During the 1850's a number of changes took place in the Sacramento Valley because of the great influx of population. The value of land increased and excellent profits could be made in supplying food to the mining regions. On July 5, 1856, William Wolfskill sold his half of Rancho Río de los Putos to Andrew Stevenson, G. B. Stevenson, Mathus Wolfskill and Edward McGary for $71,000.[48] The land did not remain for long out of the Wolfskill family hands, because on September 14, 1858, these purchasers sold their holdings, less 870 acres retained by Mathus, to John Reid Wolfskill.[49] The only portion then sold to an outsider was the additional tract purchased by Green McMahan in 1859.

By 1860 the Wolfskill brothers began to grow wheat and to fence the land. John Wolfskill and Green McMahan built twenty-one miles of fence in a single year at a cost of ten thousand dollars. Apparently John constructed the adobe house on McMahan's land in payment for his help with the fence.[50]

Throughout the latter half of the nineteenth cen-

---

[47] "A sketch of the active part . . . ," loc cit., 4.

[48] Deed of Wm. Wolfskill to A. and G. B. Stevenson, Mathus Wolfskill, and Edward McGary, July 5, 1856, in the possession of Mrs. Robert Dart.

[49] Deed of A. and G. B. Stevenson and Edward McGary to John R. Wolfskill, Sept. 14, 1858, in the possession of Mrs. Robert Dart.

[50] Wood, "Samuel Green McMahan," 295.

tury, John Reid Wolfskill was considered to be one of the leading citizens of the Sacramento Valley region.[51] He married Susan Cooper, the daughter of the Wolfskills' Madison County neighbor, Major Stephen Cooper. Susan and her father had been among the survivors of the Donner expedition to California in 1846. The John Wolfskills became the parents of a son, Edward, and three daughters, Melinda, Frances and Jennie.[52] All of these children remained in or near Solano County to become permanent residents. The Wolfskill ranch was well known for its agricultural productivity, and John Reid made several contributions in this field. On the site where he first slept in a tree to avoid grizzly bears, Wolfskill founded the town of Winters, California. John Reid Wolfskill died in 1897 and the majority of the original Río de los Putos grant was passed down to his descendants. In 1936, Frances Wolfskill Taylor left a considerable portion of the land at Winters to the University of California as an agricultural experimental station. Since that time the land has been used effectively by the state university's College of Agriculture (Davis Campus) for various orchard and vineyard experiments.[53]

51 "Solano's Pioneer Settler, Career of the Late John R. Wolfskill, the Founder of Winters," in Vacaville *Reporter,* June 5, 1897.

52 Melinda married Clay Goodyear; Frances, Samuel Taylor; and Jennie, Frank Bonney.

53 Claude B. Hutchison, ed., *California Agriculture* (Berkeley, 1946), 157.

6

California Sangria

Fresh come, to a new world indeed, yet long prepared,
I see the genius of the modern,

child of the real and ideal.
— Walt Whitman

Sangría – the popular Spanish beverage made from full-bodied red table wine, the juice of a variety of choice citrus fruits, slices of fresh bananas and peaches, a dash of light, flavorful brandy, and a bit of sugar for sweetening – typifies the contributions of William Wolfskill to California agriculture. As the Spanish *cantinero,* or innkeeper, achieved a perfect combination of ingredients in creating *sangría,* Wolfskill achieved a similar perfection in the production of these basic ingredients. As one of the outstanding pioneers in the early wine industry, as founder of the commercial orange industry, and as a cultivator of tropical and domestic fruits, Wolfskill indeed had the foresight and the skillful touch which resulted in a successful agricultural enterprise.

The planting of vineyards and orchards had long been pursued in California through the endeavors of the Spanish padres, but were not exploited until Wolfskill's day. After the Franciscans established their first mission at San Diego in 1769, they began cultivating vines brought in from Baja California to produce their necessary sacramental and other wines.

With the subsequent founding of new missions, wine-making spread northward, although the area of major concentration remained in southern California until the late 1850's. Padres particularly noted for their success in viniculture were those at San Fernando, San Gabriel and San Antonio. Today visitors to Mission San Antonio may still see the remains of the great *bodegas* or wine cellars, in which wines pressed from mission grapes were kept for future use. The Franciscans, however, concentrated all their attention on a single variety of wine-grape, somewhat mediocre in quality, which was soon called by the appropriate, if not very original, name of "Mission." [1] The reason the mission fathers failed to develop a superior type of grape was that even though they considered wine an article of commerce, they produced it mainly for their own purposes.[2] Similarly their orange orchards were planted primarily to supply the missions with citrus fruit or for distribution to various private homes. The fruits of these trees, which were planted in court-yards or gardens, were all consumed at home or given away to friends.[3]

Prior to 1830 very few grapevines were cultivated by private individuals, although in 1824 Joseph Chapman, the Yankee shipbuilder, planted 4,000 vines in a rather unsuccessful attempt to break into

[1] *Wine of California* (A.T. & S.F. Railway Co., 1937), 10.

[2] Philip M. Wagner, *A Wine-Grower's Guide* (New York, 1945), 24.

[3] J. Eliot Coit, *Citrus Fruits – An Account of the Citrus Fruit Industry with Special Reference to California Requirements and Practices* (New York, 1915), 2.

the wine industry.[4] The greatest stimulation to the industry on a private commercial basis was provided by the secularization of the missions after 1834. This act on the part of the Mexican government caused the padres to generally abandon their vineyards and orchards, and consequently to relinquish their chief source of income – the production of wine. Since grape growing and wine making had become major factors in the economy of the missions of southern California, immigrants to the territory were quick to realize the potentialities of commercial viticulture.[5]

The suitability of California and particularly Los Angeles County as a grape producing area resulted from a combination of several factors. The virgin soil and the temperate climate were ideal, and California vineyards generally yielded a much larger crop than those in other parts of the world.[6] A lack of severe storms and frost was a major factor in the success of the grape crop, and it was possible to make wine by fermentation without artificial heat during the winter. A greater variety of grapes could thrive on California soil than on soils elsewhere; and in addition to wine making, the production of raisins and table grapes proved to be a lucrative business.[7] These same conditions, especially the lack of frost,

[4] Bancroft, *History of California,* II, p. 767.

[5] Vincent P. Carosso, *The California Wine Industry, 1830-1895* (Berkeley, 1951), 7.

[6] John S. Hittell, *The Resources of California* (San Francisco, 1863), 20.

[7] T. Hart Hyatt, *Handbook of Grape Culture* (San Francisco, 1867), 20.

were the primary factors contributing to the success of the citrus industry.

One of the significant problems faced by persons engaged in agriculture in the Los Angeles area was that of water. Even Spanish Governor Felipe de Neve, who selected the pueblo site in 1777, indicated a fear that there might be some difficulty in obtaining an adequate water supply for irrigation. For this reason one of the obligations of every pueblo resident under the municipal code was to cooperate in the construction of canals and such irrigation ditches as might be necessary for the town. A water commission was set up by the *ayuntamiento* to project and direct these activities. William Wolfskill served on the *comisión de aguas* during his term as *regidor* (city councilman) during the year 1844.[8]

An indication of the manner by which the water problem was handled can be obtained from the following circular which was issued by Alcalde Stephen C. Foster's "Committee on Water Supply for the year 1848:"

> *To Owners of farming lands whose names appear on the preceding list, Greetings:*
>
> The time of putting the *zanjas* [9] (canals) in proper order having arrived and it being a matter of interest to all to have the river dam put into a condition which will make the many

---

[8] Nombrimiento de comisiones, Jan. 5, 1844. *Los Angeles Archives,* II, p. 739. Wolfskill was appointed by Alcalde Manuel Requena to serve with Juan Bandini on both the water commission and the police commission.

[9] See Henry D. Barrows, "Water for Domestic Purposes vs. Water for Irrigation," in *Annual Report of the Los Angeles County Pioneers of Southern California,* VII (1912-13), 64.

repairs resorted to every year unnecessary and which will correspondingly reduce the damages caused by a water famine . . . every person named in the above list will send to the headworks the number of laborers which he is to furnish together with the proper tools . . . to make the necessary repairs on the river dam aforesaid, failing which the guilty parties shall pay a daily fine of four *reales* (fifty cents) for each laborer missing. Orders were given by the Water Overseer not to accept boys unable to do a man's work, nor to admit any laborer with tools that cannot be used.[10]

Out of the one hundred four names on the list, which contained the names of all proprietors of town-farms in 1848, just eight were foreigners.[11] Two of these, William Wolfskill and Luis Vignes, were the only persons required to contribute four *reales* monthly toward the salary of the Water Overseer and furnish as many as three laborers. The majority were to pay two *reales* and furnish but one laborer.[12]

During the years following his first acquisition of land in 1836, Wolfskill actively pursued his interests in commercial viniculture and in the culture of citrus and tropical fruits. In several of his agricultural undertakings, Wolfskill worked closely with his friend and neighbor Jean Louis Vignes. Vignes, a Frenchman, had arrived in Monterey in 1829, and

[10] Circular, Feb. 4, 1848. *Los Angeles Archives,* IV, p. 533.

[11] Warner, *Historical Sketch of Los Angeles County,* 75, lists these as Abel Stearns, Louis Bouchet, Louis Vignes, Juan Domingo, Miguel N. Pryor, William Wolfskill, Louis Lemoreau, and Joseph Snooks.

[12] List of owners of agricultural lands in the City of Los Angeles interested in the municipal water supply, showing their proportion of the salary assigned to the Water Overseer, and the number of laborers each has to furnish, Feb. 4, 1848. *Los Angeles Archives,* IV, p. 531.

after a trip to southern California decided to settle
in the Los Angeles area. In 1831 he purchased 104
acres of land near present day Alameda and Aliso
streets for the purpose of planting a vineyard.[13] The
property would later border Wolfskill's on the south.
Don Luis, as Vignes was usually called by his Span-
ish-speaking neighbors, soon built an adobe residence,
planted a garden, and built a distillery. His rancho
became known as "El Aliso" from the incorrect
application of the Spanish word *aliso,* meaning alder,
to the large sycamore tree which shaded his home.

Vignes was not satisfied with the variety of grape
cultivated by the mission fathers and began to import
cuttings of prized French wine varieties. Several of
these, which were shipped first to Boston and then
around the Horn to California, began to produce in
large enough quantities to be used in wine making in
the early thirties.[14] By 1839 Vignes had more than
forty thousand vines thriving on his acres and had
begun to charter ships, which he loaded at San Pedro,
for regular shipments of wines and brandies to the
ports of Santa Barbara, Monterey and San Francisco.[15] In addition to his vineyard, the Frenchman
had perhaps the largest number of orange trees in
any private garden. Thirty-five trees had been trans-

13 Wagner, *A Wine-Grower's Guide,* 26; Hutchison, *California Agriculture,* 29.

14 Carosso, *California Wine Industry,* 8-9; Idwal Jones, *Vines in the
Sun* (New York, 1949), 212.

15 Wine Advisory Board, *Wine Handbook Series* (San Francisco, 1943),
7.

planted from Mission San Gabriel to his home in 1834 and the fruit was used for home consumption and distribution among friends.[16]

On June 7, 1851, Luis Vignes offered for sale his "desirable property, El Alizo" stating that there were "two orange gardens that yield from five to six thousand oranges in the season" and a vineyard of forty thousand vines which would "yield 1,000 barrels of wine per annum, the quality of which is well known to be superior." He finally sold his property to his nephew Jean Louis Sainsevain in April of 1855 for $42,000.[17] Jean Louis, who had arrived from France in 1849, joined with his brother Pierre in forming the firm of Sainsevain Bros. The brothers later became famous not only as producers of quality wine but also as pioneer wine merchants, having made their first shipment to San Francisco in 1855.[18]

The oranges in Luis Vignes' garden particularly intrigued William Wolfskill. It was his belief that this fruit, which Don Luis was growing for home use, had commercial possibilities.[19] In the year 1841 the ex-trapper from Kentucky planted the nucleus of his soon to be famous orange grove. Obtaining his trees from the mission at San Gabriel, Wolfskill set them out on a two acre site adjoining his adobe

[16] Jessie E. Boyd, *Historical Import of the Orange Industry in California* (Unpublished MA thesis, University of California, 1922), 55.

[17] Pierre Sainsevain to Arpad Haraszthy, June 2, 1886. Haraszthy Family Papers, Bancroft Library.

[18] Warner, *Historical Sketch of Los Angeles County*, 112, 114.

[19] Coit, *Citrus Fruits*, 3.

dwelling.[20] He always dated this orchard by saying it "was of the same age as his daughter Juana, who was born in 1841." [21] Wolfskill sold his fruit commercially to such an advantage that he was able to increase the size of his orchard to approximately twenty-eight acres by the early 1850's and eventually to seventy acres.[22] It is related that Wolfskill chanced to be strolling on a wharf in San Francisco in 1854 when a schooner just in from the Sandwich Islands began unloading a full cargo of Hawaiian oranges. Much of the fruit was spoiled and about to be cast overboard so Wolfskill "bought it for a song, shipped it south and had the seed extracted and sown – thus securing trees to add thirty acres to his holdings." [23]

Wolfskill seems to have intended from the very first to raise his oranges for profit. His venture proved so successful in the years following his first plantings that an official of the Orange Grower's Union was to remark at a later time that Wolfskill's profits "probably had more to do with stimulating orange growing in southern California from that time forward than any other influence." [24] His success stimulated others and there was a considerable increase in orange planting after 1850. In 1853 Matthew Keller and a Dr.

20 J. Albert Wilson, *History of Los Angeles County* (Oakland, 1880), 183, states that "Wolfskill set out about 60 or 80 trees but in 1856 had only 32 bearing trees."

21 Warner, *Historical Sketch of Los Angeles County*, 65.

22 Coit, *Citrus Fruits*, 3.

23 John L. Von Blon, "Here Oranges like Ruddy Lanterns Shine," in *Touring Topics*, XXV (November 1933), 13.

24 William A. Spaulding, "Early Chapters in the History of California Citrus Culture," in *California Citrograph*, VII (March 1922), 66.

Halsey imported some orange seeds from Central America and the Hawaiian Islands. Both planted nurseries which were later acquired by Wolfskill. Others who entered the business were Benjamin D. Wilson, who planted an orchard in the San Gabriel Valley in 1852; L. Van Leuven and L. F. Cram, pioneer orange growers of San Bernardino; and Myron H. Crafts who set out two hundred trees at Crafton in 1865.[25]

By 1854 Dr. Halsey, a frequent visitor to the Wolfskill home, had planted his orange nursery on land which had originally belonged to John Rowland, grantee with William Workman of La Puente Rancho.[26] Halsey's tract was located along the San Gabriel River, eleven or twelve miles east of Los Angeles, and was always known as "The Rowland Place." The land, which also contained a sizable lemon nursery, was purchased by William Wolfskill in August of 1855 for the sum of four thousand dollars. He purchased additional land during the same month to extend his orange orchard.[27] In April of 1857, when there were probably not more than one hundred orange trees bearing fruit in the entire county,[28] Wolfskill planted several thousand trees

[25] Ludwig Louis Salvator, "A Flower from the Golden Land," in *Touring Topics*, XXI (January 1929), 19.

[26] John Rowland and William Workman had led an expedition from New Mexico to California over the Old Spanish Trail in 1841. They were granted the forty-eight thousand acre rancho in the San Gabriel Valley in 1843.

[27] H. D. Barrows, "Diary," Aug. 9, 1855.

[28] The majority of trees on Wolfskill's seventy acres were not yet bearing fruit.

and thus established what was to be, for that time,
the largest orange orchard in the United States.[29]
Wolfskill found it necessary to discard many of the
lemon trees received from Halsey because of frost-
bite, but he replanted 1800 good ones which had survived a severe freeze of 1849 and was able to cultivate
an extensive lemon crop.[30] The Los Angeles *Star*
reported in October of 1857 that in addition to the
2,000 young orange trees which he had transplanted
the previous spring, Wolfskill had quite a number of
lime and lemon trees and numerous "citron trees,
heavily laden with their fragrant fruit." [31]

There was considerable demand during the late
1850's for California citrus fruits because of a scurvy
epidemic in the state of Sonora, Mexico. Wolfskill
was able to take advantage of this demand by supplying his thick-skinned seedling lemons, which at that
time had a "longer shipping life" than oranges. He
then became the competitor of John Sutter, Jr., who
had established an extensive lemon and lime orchard
at Acapulco, Mexico, for shipment to California.
Wolfskill is also supposed to have broken the fresh
citrus monopoly of Queen Pomari of Papeete, Ta-
hiti.[32]

Wolfskill had been fortunate in keeping his
oranges and other citrus fruits free from the attacks

29 Newmark, *Sixty Years in Southern California,* 211.

30 A. J. Lorenz, *Centennial of the California Lemon* (Los Angeles, 1949), 2.

31 Los Angeles *Star,* Oct. 24, 1857.

32 Lorenz, *Centennial of the California Lemon,* 3, from notes and letters preserved by Mrs. Robert Cooper, grand-daughter of William Wolfskill.

of insects or other damaging parasites during the first fifteen years. In 1856 the total yield for Los Angeles County was estimated at one hundred thousand oranges and Wolfskill averaged from each of his thirty-two bearing trees a net yield of one hundred dollars per annum.[33] But in 1857-'58-'59 came the white or fluted scale which injured the trees and destroyed the crop. Through research carried on by the Wolfskills, local scientists and the California Department of Agriculture, a means was discovered by which it could be combatted.[34] The tiny insect had caused an almost total crop failure until 1862, when a fair yield was again realized. In that year John S. Hittell in his *Resources of California* estimated the total number of orange trees planted in the state to be two thousand five hundred with "more than two-thirds being in the orchard of William Wolfskill at Los Angeles." [35]

Frost-bite occurred from time to time but did not constitute a serious threat to the orchards. Another of Nature's whims, however, did raise sufficient havoc to warrant mention in the local newspaper. On February 7, 1865, an article appeared which described a "Santa Ana" wind which had "swept over the valley with remorseless fury . . . raising such clouds of dust and sand that nearly every merchant in town was compelled to close his place of

[33] Wilson, *History of Los Angeles County*, 63.
[34] Henry Barrows, "Letter from Los Angeles," in Los Angeles *Star*, Oct. 24, 1859.
[35] Hittell, *Resources of California*, 197.

business . . ." and causing much damage to the
orange orchards of the city and vicinity. "The trees
were loaded with fruit at the time, which was blown
off and injured beyond sale; the trees are also much
damaged and in many instances entirely ruined. We
understand that Mr. Wolfskill estimates his loss in
fruit and trees as high as $500. . ." [36]

Among the early visitors to the Wolfskill home in
Los Angeles was Edwin Bryant, an American traveler
who visited the ranch in 1847. Bryant commented
that the glass of wine which he was served "com-
pared favorably with the best French and Madeira
wines." He was also impressed with the vineyard, the
orchard and the "Old Adobe" itself, observing that it

> . . . was a delightful recreation to stroll through it and
> among the tropical fruit trees bordering its walks. His house,
> too, exhibited an air of cleanliness and comfort and con-
> venience not often met with in this country. [37]

Wolfskill's distillery, which had been enlarged in
1843, was primarily used for the production of
brandy from the grape and other kinds of fruit. [38]
With the coming of the gold rush, many persons
would stop at the Wolfskill residence and carry
word of the extensive orchards and "fine brandy" to
the northern part of the state.

By 1851 Wolfskill was the owner of a respectable
1,100 acres in Los Angeles County assessed at

36 Los Angeles *Tri-Weekly News*, Feb. 7, 1865.

37 Edwin Bryant, *What I Saw in California: Being the Journal of a
Tour in the Years 1846 and 1847* (New York, 1848), 412.

38 Juan Temple to James McKinlay, Sept. 10, 1843. *Vallejo Documents*, XXXIII, no. 257, Bancroft Library.

$10,000. Some leading property holders were José Sepulveda with 102,000 acres assessed at $83,000; John Temple, 20,000 acres at $79,000; Abel Stearns, 14,000 acres at $90,000 and John Rowland with 29,000 acres assessed at $70,000.[39] In 1852 the Los Angeles *Star* published a list of forty-nine persons in the county who paid taxes of $100 or more. Wolfskill just made the list by paying $114 while his neighbor Luis Vignes paid $229. The four highest were John Temple, $912; José Sepulveda, $723; Abel Stearns, $719; and Antonio María Lugo, $676.[40] Six years later William Wolfskill would jump to third place on the list.

A frequent visitor at the Wolfskill ranch during the 1850's was Mrs. Emily C. Hayes, wife of Judge Benjamin Hayes. In a letter to her sister written on February 28, 1852, Mrs. Hayes gave an interesting account of her first visit to the "Old Adobe." "After attending Church," she wrote,

I walked out to a vineyard half a mile from the city. While there I ate two oranges and some dried grapes. Quite a treat to get to such a place. They have all kinds of fruit trees and twenty thousand grape vines. The peaches and quinces are in bloom and the orange trees full of oranges. They look beautiful indeed. The gentlemen (Mr. Wm. Wolfskill) who owns the place is from Missouri; left there many years since; has a Californian wife. He was not at home, but his wife is very agreeable. We bought two dozen oranges, paying her one dollar.[41]

[39] Warner, *Historical Sketch of Los Angeles County*, 80.
[40] Los Angeles *Star*, July 17, 1852.
[41] Emily C. Hayes to a sister, Feb. 28, 1852. Bancroft, "Biographical Scraps: Benjamin Hayes," Bancroft Library.

According to Judge Hayes' diary, he and his wife called upon the Wolfskills many times in the following years. A note on September 10, 1857, indicates that they had gone out "to Wolfskill's for peaches" but that there were very few that season. They "got the last." Judge Hayes also wrote that "Emily walked there this morning, and was improved by the long walk," that Wolfskill had cut down a large number of worn-out peach trees, seventeen years old, to make room for oranges, and that "he gave Emily a bottle of the pure juice of the grape." [42]

William Wolfskill had planted a number of different kinds of fruits both for commercial and experimental purposes. A news item in the *Star* of August 20, 1853 reported that the arrival of the steamer "Goliath" had increased the activity of local fruit-growers and that Alexander & Banning's six teams had taken 350 packages of fruit down to San Pedro. Included among the largest shippers was H. C. Cardwell "from Wolfskill's orchard with 98 packages containing 3,014 lbs. of peaches, 487 lbs. apples and 136 lbs. pears." [43] In 1855 Henry F. Teschemacher, a former mayor of San Francisco, brought William Wolfskill some sweet almonds from the Mediterranean area. From these Wolfskill planted and successfully raised quite an extensive almond orchard; but even though the soft-shelled almond grew well and maintained an excellent flavor, the

---

[42] Benjamin Hayes, "Notes on California Affairs," MS 57, Bancroft Library.

[43] Los Angeles *Star,* Aug. 20, 1853.

trees did not produce enough to make their culture profitable. In later years Luis Wolfskill raised the Languedoc variety on a larger scale but with similar discouraging results.[44]

Speaking of the year 1855, Harris Newmark wrote that two partially successful attempts were made that year to introduce the chestnut tree. According to Newmark, a resident of Los Angeles since 1853, "William Wolfskill, who first brought here the persimmon-tree," took some seeds of an Italian variety of chestnut which Solomon Lazard had imported from Bordeaux and planted them near his homestead.[45] Juan José Warner reported that Wolfskill afterwards gave two of the trees to his son-in-law Henry Cardwell. Cardwell's land was eventually acquired by Ozro W. Childs and the trees, later "large and productive" could be seen at the Childs' residence.[46] Cardwell himself introduced seedling strawberries to Los Angeles in January of 1856.[47]

Continuing to make improvements on his land, William Wolfskill was awarded a diploma at the 1856 State Fair in San Jose for having the best vineyard in California, and was awarded a snuff-box by the California State Agricultural Society for producing the best lemons and grapes.[48] An article appearing in the Wilmington *Journal* in 1857 stated

[44] Warner, *Historical Sketch of Los Angeles County*, 77.

[45] Newmark, *Sixty Years in Southern California*, 125.

[46] Warner, *Historical Sketch of Los Angeles County*, 77.

[47] Los Angeles *Star*, July 7, 1856.

[48] Items in the possession of John C. Wolfskill, grandson of William Wolfskill.

that "H. D. Barrows of Los Angeles . . . sailing for the east tomorrow, is taking on a barrel of Los Angeles wine to President Buchanan from the celebrated Wolfskill Vineyard. He also bears with him as California offerings to the President samples of the various semi-tropical productions of the southern portion of the State, such as oranges, lemons, citrons, almonds, walnuts, grapes, etc." [49]

The paper later reported that Mr. Barrows "had called on President Buchanan with various specimens of California wines and fruits, which he brought from the Pacific side for that purpose." The offerings consisted of a barrel of "fine old California port, made by Mr. Wolfskill from his own vineyard, probably the largest in California"; two cases of white and red wines, grape brandy, Angelica wine, and "a half a dozen other brands all grown and made by Don Manuel Requena." [50]

During the year of 1858 a committee from the California State Agricultural Society visited all of the orchards, vineyards and cultivated fields in the state, making a detailed report on each of these. The committee visited the farm of John and Sarchel Wolfskill in the north and stated that they had cultivated some 280 acres which were half grain and half orchard and vineyard, and that the farm had "Chinese Chestnut, four years old, in bearing, the only one in the state." [51] The committee's report on

---

49 "California Offerings to President Buchanan," in Wilmington *Journal*, April 24, 1857. These fruits were from Wolfskill's orchards.

50 "Products of California," in *ibid.*, June 3, 1857.

the activities of William Wolfskill in Los Angeles contained nothing but praise. In addition to the facts that the vineyard consisted of 100 acres with 60,000 vines and the orchard contained 2,200 orange, lemon and lime trees, the visitors commented as follows:

> . . . trees planted in a style of exact neatness seldom equaled. It presents a sight which of its kind, is quite superior to anything in the state. We have never seen quinces equaling those on his place. We were here also shown an immense fig-tree, whose branches had drooped to the ground and taken root, like the Banyan Trees of the Indies, forming one of the most perfect bowers conceivable. Mr. Wolfskill is now paying great attention to the cultivation of choice varieties of peach, apple, pear, plum and cherry trees, many of which are now in fruit. Perhaps no man in the fruit business of this state has realized a more complete and satisfactory success than the proprietor of this place.[52]

Also in the year 1858 an article appeared in the San Francisco *Daily Evening Bulletin* entitled "Wolfskill's Vineyard and Orchard at Los Angeles" which gave a considerable amount of detail regarding Wolfskill's operations. An idea of the multiplicity of his activities, as well as the degree of knowledge and skill Wolfskill possessed in the field of agriculture, can be gained from the information presented therein. In addition to some vineyard statistics, the article listed a complete inventory of the orchard and nursery:

---

[51] "Report of the Visiting Committee," *Transactions of the California State Agricultural Society for 1858* (Sacramento, 1859), 239.

[52] *Ibid.*, 287.

. . . There are here thirty orange trees bearing; most of which are about 19 years old, from the seed; 2,050 in orchard but not in fruit and 4,000 are in the nursery; lime trees in orchard 23, in nursery 6,000; six citron trees in fruit and 100 in nursery; walnut trees in bearing 61, in nursery 300; bearing apricot trees 18 (embracing 12 varieties), in nursery 40; of pear trees in bearing there are 60 in fruit of 11 varieties and 60 comprising 20 varieties not in bearing, and 100 in nursery.

The apple trees in bearing are 400 of 15 varieties. There are 12 quince trees and four olive trees in bearing and six of the latter not yet in fruit. Of lemon trees there are 66 in the orchard and 100 in the nursery; 30 fig trees in fruit, 10 not yet bearing and 50 in nursery embracing many varieties.

Of the orange trees in fruit, some have produced as many as 1,000 in a season and one of the trees not less than 2,000; which at 6½ cents each makes the handsome little sum of $125.00 as the product of one tree. Within the past year the trees have been attacked by an insect that is proving very destructive to the oranges.

The article also furnished suggestions on how to irrigate a vineyard and to prune the vines. It mentioned Wolfskill's residence and stated that there were four wine cellars located on the place with a capacity for storing 60,000 gallons of wine with convenience, and when necessary the entire capacity could be used to store 100,000 gallons. It described Wolfskill's distillery as occupying part of an extensive modern brick building and producing brandies which "have been in request by the lovers of California brandy." In conclusion the account of Wolfskill's vineyard and orchard offered the following:

There is also upon these grounds a Willow grove planted by William Wolfskill which occupies a number of acres furnishing poles for fencing and some firewood. The quantity of grapes sent to market as well as of wine and brandy made from the vineyard must be referred to a future number.[53]

Before fruit was raised to any great extent in the central and northern part of the state, and even some times during the sixties, Wolfskill and other Los Angeles vineyardists, including John Rowland, Benjamin D. Wilson, the Sainsevain brothers and others, shipped large quantities of grapes to San Francisco. These grapes in 1851 and '52 brought twenty cents per pound in the city and as much as seventy-five or eighty cents in the interior.[54] Arpad Haraszthy, son of the famous pioneer wine producer Agoston Haraszthy, reported that in 1852 and '53 grapes selling in and around Los Angeles on the vines for two to six cents per pound brought from fifty cents to one dollar in San Francisco, as there was no one there to supply the demand.[55] By August of 1854 the "first installment of grapes in merchantable quantities" was received at Sacramento from the Wolfskill ranch

[53] San Francisco *Daily Evening Bulletin*, Dec. 17, 1858.

[54] Warner, *Historical Sketch of Los Angeles County*, 113.

[55] "Wine Making in California," in *Overland Monthly*, VII (Dec. 1871), 490. A Hungarian immigrant, Agoston Haraszthy, is sometimes considered the "father of the California wine industry." Arriving in San Diego in 1849, and later moving to the north, Haraszthy experimented with numerous foreign wine varieties which he introduced throughout the state after 1850. His period of greatest activity was in the late 1850's in Sonoma County, where he planted 85,556 vines of approximately 165 varieties. His son Arpad became one of the founders of the champagne industry in the state and was a member of the Buena Vista Vinicultural Society after 1862.

on Putah Creek. "They were of the ordinary blue variety, weighed 250 lbs. and were sold at $1.25 per lb." [56] From that time forward northern vineyardists began to offer serious competition to southern producers. Wolfskill, however, had interests in both regions.

During the grape season of 1857, according to records kept by "the great forwarding house of P. Banning at San Pedro," 21,000 boxes of grapes, averaging 45 pounds each, were shipped to San Francisco; and at times William Wolfskill shipped as many as five hundred boxes of grapes on a single steamer. But even with the rising market for grapes, Wolfskill continued his wine-making activities.[57] His vintage of 1857 was reported in the Los Angeles *Star* as "12,000 gallons wine, 2,000 gallons angelica, two or three hundred gallons brandy and 150,000 pounds of grapes, shipped to San Francisco." Angelica was a popular "ladies wine" described as "a sweet liquor, or wine, admirably designed to please the palate, but producing 'the largest sized' headache on those who indulged in it too liberally." It was made by adding "one gallon of grape brandy to three gallons of unfermented grape juice" and allowing a slight fermentation to take place. If bottled it became somewhat sparkling. The *Star* warned that it was "a most palatable and agreeable drink, but woe to him who drinks too deeply." [58]

56 Los Angeles *Star*, Aug. 24, 1854.
57 Warner, *Historical Sketch of Los Angeles County*, 114.
58 Los Angeles *Star*, Oct. 24, 1857.

ORANGE GROVES OF WILLIAM WOLFSKILL IN LOS ANGELES

BANANA TREES NEAR THE "OLD ADOBE" IN LOS ANGELES

Both of the above photographs are reproduced by courtesy of the
Historical Collections, Security First National Bank, Los Angeles.

View showing Orange and Lemon Groves and Residence of Joseph W. Wolfs
between Alameda and San Pedro Streets, Los Angeles, California

From Thompson and West's *Los Angeles County*, 1889.

Award to William Wolfskill for the Best Vineyard in 1856

An idea of the value of the vineyards in southern California during this period can be gained from the Los Angeles County Assessor's returns for 1858 as corrected by the Board of Equalization. Those tax-payers whose property was assessed at $10,000 or more were listed as the "Wealthy Men of the County" in the *Southern Vineyard*.[59] William Wolf-skill's property was given an assessed valuation of $80,000, third highest in the county; the Sainsevain Brothers, $40,000; John Rowland, $35,712; and Matthew Keller, $34,325. The two men with the largest assessments, Abel Stearns and John Temple with $186,586 and $89,556 respectively, were engaged in enterprises which included valuable business holdings.[60]

A large portion of the grape yield in southern California was purchased by the firm of Kohler and Frohling, an established wine house in San Francisco since 1848. These two men had fled Germany after the upheaval in 1848 and had come to America as musicians. Kohler, who organized the German Concert Society in San Francisco, was responsible for the marketing of the wines in the city, while Frohling, a flutist, manufactured them in Los Angeles.[61] When the German musicians lost in wine ventures,

---

[59] Sept. 18, 1858. *The Southern Vineyard* was a newspaper founded on March 20, 1858 by J. J. Warner. The press and material formerly belonged to the *Southern Californian* in which Warner had an interest. On June 8, 1860, the *Southern Vineyard* ceased publication, and the plant was transferred to the Los Angeles *News*.

[60] The firm of Lazard & Wolfskill, in which Timothy Wolfskill was in partnership with Solomon Lazard, was assessed at $15,000.

[61] Jones, *Vines in the Sun*, 241.

they played in theaters until they had saved enough money to get back into the business. By 1857, however, the firm of Kohler and Frohling was established on a sound basis and the volume was sufficient to warrant the hiring of a wagon and team of horses on a full-time basis.[62] By this time they had also acquired a number of their own vineyards and were well known in southern California. In January of 1858 the Los Angeles Vineyard Society, of which they were members, began extensive plantings in the area of Anaheim, and many of the cuttings for the new vineyards were obtained from vines on Wolfskill's land.[63]

From a total production in 1856 of 15,000 gallons, Kohler and Frohling produced more than 100,000 gallons of wine from the vintage of 1858. By 1860, the firm had shipped over $70,000 worth of wine outside of California and had established a branch office in New York.[64] Besides the produce from their 22,000 bearing vines in Los Angeles, they annually purchased the grape crop of more than 350 acres of Los Angeles vineyards, which they stored in the cellars of the City Hall as well as at those located at William Wolfskill's. During the picking season they employed an average of 150 men to pick, crush and prepare the wine for fermentation.[65]

---

[62] *Ibid.*, 242.

[63] Henry D. Barrows, "Two Notable Pioneers – Col. J. J. Ayers and Geo. Hansen," in *Annual Publications of the Historical Society of Southern California*, IV (1897), 58.

[64] *Cozzens' Wine Press*, I (Jan. 20, 1859) in Carosso, *California Wine Industry*, p. 32.

Kohler and Frohling bought the grapes from the vineyards of Wolfskill, John Rowland,[66] Antonio Coronel, Matthew Keller and others for about three cents a pound, and the firm was entitled to use the wine cellars and presses located on the property of the various grape producers.[67] In a column entitled "Letter from Los Angeles" which appeared weekly in the San Francisco *Daily Evening Bulletin,* Henry D. Barrows took this opportunity to describe the process of wine-making at Wolfskill's vineyard as it was carried on by Kohler and Frohling in 1859. Barrows used Wolfskill's vineyard because it was representative of the general mode of operation in Los Angeles at the time, and said the following about the wine-making process:

> . . . They employ about 40 hands, two-thirds of whom are engaged in picking and hauling in the grapes; the balance are at work about the presses or in the cellars. The grapes are cut off by the stem from the vine and carried in baskets to the crossroads running through the vineyard and turned into tubs holding from 150 to 200 pounds (or as large as two men can easily handle) which are hauled in one-horse carts to the press where they are weighed, and then turned into a large "hopper" which has an apron or strong wire sieve, through which they are "stemmed," [68]

[65] Charles Kohler, "Wine Production in California," ms, Bancroft Library.

[66] John Rowland had planted extensive vineyards on his portion of Rancho La Puente and sold large quantities of wine which he produced commercially throughout the 1850's and 60's.

[67] Barrows, "Story of an Old Pioneer," in Los Angeles *World,* Oct. 7, 1887.

[68] Henry D. Barrows, "Letter from Los Angeles," in San Francisco *Daily Evening Bulletin,* Oct. 24, 1859.

It was generally the practice of European wine makers to use a stemmer with a wooden grating because most of the baser metals were corroded by the acid of the grape. Californians, however, seemed to favor the wire grating.[69] After the stems were thrown out, the next step was to mash the grape. This was done, in the words of Barrows,

> . . . when the latter is run through a mill consisting of two grooved iron cylanders [sic] so gauged as to run as closely as possible together without mashing the seeds. The grooves of one cylinder are longitudinal and of the other spiral. This method is quicker, less laborious and far more decent than the old way of "treading out" the grapes, which in a measure has passed away, as it should.
>
> Although this method (treading with bare feet) is as old as the hills and is still followed in many extensive wine-growing countries, allow me to suggest through your columns, as a good field for Yankee ingenuity to spread itself, the invention of the best machine for mashing grapes for making wine. The machine described above in most respects, however, works admirably – better than any other I ever saw. By it the mere crushing of the grape is done by two men more easily than probably ten men could do the same work by any of the old methods of tramping, malls, or what not.[70]

In regard to the crushing of the grapes, E. H. Rixford commented that "many of the best writers of today (1883) are of the opinion that the wine is better when the grapes have been well trodden with the bare feet . . . ," but continued by saying

---

[69] E. H. Rixford, *The Wine Press and the Cellar* (San Francisco, 1883), 23.

[70] Barrows, "Letter from Los Angeles," in Los Angeles *Star,* Oct. 24, 1859.

that Californians, in contrast to many Europeans, regarded treading as an antiquated practice and a relic of the past. He further surmised that "those who are fastidious in this matter may rest assured, that if they will drink California wine, they run but very small risk of imbibing a liquid which a man has had his feet in." [71]

On the other hand, Harris Newmark recalled a somewhat different method used to make wine in the early days and described the part taken by the Indians:

> Stripped to the skin, and wearing only loin-cloths, they tramped with ceaseless tread from morn till night, pressing from the luscious fruit of the vineyard the juice so soon to ferment into wine. . .

He continued to explain that the grapes were placed in elevated vats so that the liquid could run into connecting vessels and that the entire process exhaled a stale acidity which scented the air. Newmark concluded with the comment that the high southern California temperature coupled with the incessant toil of the Indians "caused the perspiration to drip from their swarthy bodies into the wine product, the sight of which in no wise increased my appetite for California wine." [72] Actually treading "by feet" was a common practice as late as 1857 as evidenced by an article in the Los Angeles *Star* which stated that "in the manufacture of wine at this [Wolfskill's] vineyard, the grapes, as they come from

[71] Rixford, *The Wine Press and the Cellar,* 23.
[72] Newmark, *Sixty Years in Southern California,* 202.

the vineyard are thrown into a large shallow vat, where half a dozen persons rapidly mash the grapes by treading them." [73] By the 1860's, however, various machines and processes had been invented for the purpose of crushing and expressing the juice from the grape. A popular one consisted of India rubber-covered cylinders which crushed the berry without breaking the seed.[74]

In his *Bulletin* letter, Barrows described exactly what happened to the grapes as they were being converted into wine. After being ground, the pommace was allowed to run down into a vat, on the bottom of which was a grating through which the juice of the grape could run. This liquid was then conveyed into tubs for white wines. The pommace was "taken directly into spiral screw presses and subjected to moderate pressure, the runnings from which made pale or yellow wine, like sherry." The grape skins were put into large tubs to ferment six or eight days or longer, for red wine, "when the residue of their vinous property" was "extracted in aguardientes by distillation.[75]

The process of fermentation followed in these early days generally consisted of pouring the juice, or must, into large casks, usually holding about 140 gallons each, until they contained about 115 gallons of liquid. A considerable surface of the wine was

[73] Los Angeles *Star,* Oct. 24, 1857.

[74] Hyatt, *Handbook of Grape Culture,* 201.

[75] Barrows, "Letter from Los Angeles," in Los Angeles *Star,* Oct. 24, 1859.

left exposed to the air in order to favor fermentation. The process began in three or four days and the period of greatest activity was completed in another three or four. The maintenance of the temperature at the proper degree of 65° F. was of great importance in preventing spoilage. The wine-maker poured in six or eight gallons of fresh juice every day until the cask was full, and then the long process of aging began. The casks were generally stored in cellars although at times they were sent on long sea voyages to complete the aging of the wine.[76]

At the vineyard of William Wolfskill, Mr. Frohling directed the activities of his workers. These men were divided into various groups and each had a particular task to perform. In this way they were able to complete the wine-making process in the least amount of time. Frohling's system was reported by Barrows as follows:

> . . . He has in his employ four men who are cleaning off the stems; this they do by pushing the grapes through the sifter with their hands; two men turn the mill by cranks; two feed the hopper; one weighs the grapes; three or four attend to the wine as it comes from the mill and the presses; five or six do the pressing and carry off the pommace to the fermenting vats; one, two or three attend to washing, cleansing and sulphuring of grapes; and three teams are constantly employed in hauling in the grapes. Every night all the presses and appliances used about them are all washed thoroughly to prevent acidity. Everything that comes in contact with the

[76] Hittell, *Resources of California*, 202-04; Bancroft, *History of California*, III, p. 49.

grape juice from the time the grape is bruised till it reaches
the cask is kept as pure as an abundance of water and hard
scrubbing can make it.[77]

The amount of wine produced by this method in
one week was considerable. Frohling and his employees turned 160,000 pounds or eighty tons of
grapes into wine at Wolfskill's vineyard in five days.
The amount of wine which these grapes yielded was
about 10,000 gallons, exclusive of a balance left in
pommace for approximately 2,000 gallons of brandy.

Further in his article Barrows cited the progress
of work at other vineyards and remarked that Frohling had finished making wine out at "Puente" the
previous week at both Mr. Workman's and Mr.
Rowland's vineyards. During the present week he
would commence "on his own and Mr. Coronel's
vineyards besides continuing operations at Mr.
Wolfskill's place where he is half done." For the
vinification Frohling employed "something over 60
men." [78]

In 1859, which was reported as an unfavorable
season, the total vintage for the state was 340,000
gallons of wine. William Wolfskill produced 50,000
gallons or nearly fifteen percent of the total. He
produced approximately five hundred barrels of
aguardiente (pure grape brandy) which held about
nineteen gallons each and usually sold for $35.00.
In "thirsty seasons" the price rose as high as $75.00.[79]

[77] Barrows, "Letter from Los Angeles," in Los Angeles *Star*, Oct. 24, 1859.

[78] *Ibid.*

[79] Wilson, *History of Los Angeles County*, 65.

In this same year Wolfskill marketed 449,000 pounds of grapes at a value of $337,000.[80] But 1859 was not merely profitable for Wolfskill, it also brought him further recognition for the quality of his vineyard. At the State Fair he was awarded a framed diploma and $30.00 for the best vineyard, second prize for the best specimens of California grapes (Matthew Keller received first prize), $25.00 for the best three dozen oranges, $35.00 for the best orange and walnut groves, and $5.00 for an exhibit of citrons and lemons.[81]

During the 1860's Wolfskill continued his agricultural activities with the help of his sons Joseph and Luis. John S. Hittell lists the Wolfskill vineyards as having 85,000 vines in his statistics for the year 1862.[82] With the expansion of the local vineyards and the planting of new ones, residents of the county finally organized the "Los Angeles Grape-Growers' and Wine-makers' Society" in October of 1866. This was the year in which Los Angeles County produced over one million gallons of wine. The Society's officers did not, however, include William Wolfskill, for he had passed away a few days before its first meeting.[83]

Joseph Wolfskill conducted extensive experiments in his father's orange orchard and succeeded in increasing the yield of the citrus trees. The last crop of oranges disposed of during William Wolfskill's life-

---

[80] Benjamin Hayes, "Notes on California Affairs," MS 71, Bancroft Library.
[81] Los Angeles *Star,* Nov. 1, 1859.
[82] Hittell, *Resources of California,* 91.
[83] Wilson, *History of Los Angeles County,* 66.

time sold on the trees for $25,000.[84] When the Cottony cushion scale, a plant parasite introduced from Australia, began to attack California orange groves during the 1870's, a representative from the United States Department of Agriculture conducted his investigation with Joseph's cooperation at the orchard bordering Alameda Street.[85] The younger Wolfskill is also given credit for sending in 1877 the first trainload of oranges to eastern markets via the recently completed Southern Pacific Railroad. The oranges, which were planted by his father, arrived in St. Louis in good condition after having been a month in transit.[86] It is said that Joseph used paper wrappings and ice, the ice having required replacement eleven times en route. The arrangements for the shipment by rail were made by Leland Stanford personally, who with his wife and son visited the Wolfskill home and orchard. The freight charges on the original boxes, which held 150 oranges each, were $500, and Wolfskill still made a good profit. This marked the opening of the citrus industry to export, and increased profits were made possible through the new rail facilities.[87]

---

[84] Coit, *Citrus Fruits,* 3.　　　　　[86] Coit, *Citrus Fruits,* 3.

[85] The parasite, known as the *Icerya purchasi,* was finally combatted by the introduction into California of its natural enemy, the Australian ladybird beetle, *Novius cardinalis,* in the 1890's. An experimental laboratory was set up on the Wolfskill ranch under the direction of Professor D. W. Coquillett.

[87] Randall H. Hewitt, "Orange Packing and Shipping," in *Annual Report of the Los Angeles County Pioneers of Southern California,* VII (1912-13), 69. Hewitt arrived in Los Angeles in 1876 and designed a new type of orange box with dividing center pieces for Joseph Wolfskill.

When President Rutherford B. Hayes visited California on his tour of 1880 he was taken "to the rural outskirts" of Los Angeles to view Wolfskill's orchards and other ranches. Joseph Wolfskill, reported the *Herald,* "had erected at the entrance of his suburban estate an arch of evergreens with the monogram 'H' " and had attached small flags to the citrus branches along the drive leading to the main groves. "The visitors got a thrill common to later tourists" when they were driven close enough to the large orange trees to be able to "pick the golden fruit from their carriage." [88]

In 1886 there appeared an announcement in the Santa Ana *Herald* that "in the Wolfskill orchard is a new orange, which promises to become a great favorite with the growers." This was the Valencia, a summer orange which would be found to thrive in no other part of the United States but California.[89]

[88] Los Angeles *Herald,* Oct. 24, 1880; Los Angeles *Daily Commercial,* Oct. 26, 1880.

[89] Santa Ana *Herald,* June 20, 1886.

Southern California in Transition

But more in you than these, lands of the Western shore.
I see in you, certain to come, the promise
of thousands of years, till now deferr'd.
Promis'd to be fulfill'd, our common kind, the race.
— Walt Whitman

The Bear Flag Republic, created on June 14, 1846, by a handful of patriotic California settlers, came to an abrupt end when United States troops raised the American flag over Monterey in July of the same year. The war with Mexico was no longer a matter for speculation. In August of 1846 Commodore Robert F. Stockton's men marched across the Sepulveda and Domínguez ranchos into Los Angeles and seized the area. John Temple was appointed alcalde of the city. On September 19, 1846, William Wolfskill took an oath of "faithful allegiance to the United States of North America" and agreed to perform the duties of "Regidor or common Councillor in the Ciudad de los Angeles without fear, favor or affection" under such laws as might be enacted by the Congress of the United States with regard to the Territory of California.[1]

The year 1846 had begun peacefully in Los An-

[1] Oath of William Wolfskill witnessed by Edward Gilchrist, Surgeon of the California Batallion, who became "Justice of the Peace in the Ciudad de Los Angeles," Sept. 19, 1846. Archibald Hamilton Gillespie Papers, Special Collections Library, University of California, Los Angeles.

geles and there was little indication of the difficulties that were brewing in the northern part of the state. Just the year before Governor Pío Pico had established his headquarters on the *Calle Principal* and local residents enjoyed the city's status as capital of California, albeit for only a few weeks. The transactions of the *ayuntamiento* continued to include routine matters and showed little departure from the ordinary course of events. For example, on January 31, 1846, "Guillermo Guisquiel" was finally granted a confirmation of title to land which he had held in dispute with Lemuel Carpenter. Even though Carpenter had built a house and planted a vineyard on the property, it was adjuged to be a part of Wolfskill's original tract.[2]

On February 19, 1846, a group of twenty-six citizens including Wolfskill, Carpenter, Richard Laughlin, Nathaniel Pryor, Antonio Coronel, Felipe Lugo and others were represented by Francisco Figueroa and Luis Vignes in a petition to Governor Pío Pico to do something about the "vulgar and mean" Indians dwelling on the nearby *ranchería*. They complained that stricter supervision should be maintained over the conduct of the Indians who came into town on Saturdays to engage in "fiestas bacanales." These pueblo residents felt that such drunken parties did nothing but spread disease and would eventually result in the complete degeneration of the Indians involved. They also recommended that

---

2 Report on the Petition of William Wolfskill, Jan. 31, 1846. *Los Angeles Archives*, II, p. 1005.

polygamy be prohibited in order to stop what amounted to prostitution.[3] Governor Pico turned the matter over to the *ayuntamiento,* under whose jurisdiction it fell, and on May 2, 1846, the city council ordered that the *ranchería* be placed "under the supervision of an honest warden" who, instructed to "moderate the customs, would thereby avoid crimes." This, however, would "not prevent the authorities from being vigilant."[4]

Not only was the conduct of the Indians causing concern, but in April of 1846, one of the members of the *ayuntamiento,* second Alcalde José L. Sepulveda, became deeply distressed by the manner in which the city council itself had been functioning. To Sepulveda this was one of the most serious problems faced by the council at that time and his appeal to fellow members reflected his anxiety:

> Until today, I have been observing with sadness that the Very Illustrious Ayuntamiento, to which I have the honor of belonging, conducts itself like a body without a soul, or a ship without a rudder, and has no fixed rules for its meetings or duties. This results in the paralyzation of its business, the discredit of the municipal body and finally in disorder in the offices of the commissions.[5]

In order to correct the situation and to establish some regulations for the conduct of business, Sepulveda proposed a total of fifty-one articles included

---

[3] Petition of Francisco Figueroa and Luis Vignes, Feb. 19, 1846. *Ibid.,* I, p. 527; II, p. 717.

[4] *Ibid.,* I, p. 530.

[5] Proyecto de reglamento presentado por el Sr. Alcalde 2⁰, April 4, 1846. *Ibid.,* II, pp. 1063-64.

in nine separate chapters. The majority contained standard recommendations for municipal procedure, but some seemed to indicate a certain degree of laxity previously enjoyed by council members. The *ayuntamiento* was to meet every day promptly at nine and members were not to leave until the conclusion of the session. They were to maintain the decency and moderation which corresponded to a council of a respectable pueblo; they were to maintain silence and composure in the sessions, speaking only in turn and without interrupting another speaker; they were not to smoke; and they could not even leave the meeting for "alguna necesidad corporal" without asking permission from the president. They would continue to meet in the Court House until the Town Hall was built and at the first opportunity a canopy was to be placed on the wall with the national colors affixed so the meetings could be held under the same. When the council members attended an official function, they were to wear black suits in order to lend dignity to the occasion.[6] The *Reglamento* proposed by Sepulveda was adopted in substance and later appeared in the American period as the Rules and Regulations for the Interior Government of the Illustrious Ayuntamiento of the City of Los Angeles.[7]

The events of the summer of 1846 which had allowed the American force to enter Los Angeles with little resistance were, by the end of September, a thing of the past. Angered by the strict discipline

[6] *Ibid.,* 1067.
[7] June 22, 1849, *Ibid.,* VII, p. 349.

I William Woolfskill, do most solemnly swear that I will bear true and faithful allegiance to the United States of North America, that I will to the best of my abilities perform the duty of Regidor or common Councillor in the Ciudad de los Angeles without fear, favor or affection & that I will be governed by such laws as are, or may hereafter be, enacted by the Congress of the United States, or by the Constituted Authorities of the Territory of California.

William Wolfskill

Sworn and Subscribed before me, Edward Gilchrist, Justice of the Peace, in this Ciudad de los Angeles this nineteenth day of September, one thousand and eight hundred and forty-six

Edward Gilchrist

WILLIAM WOLFSKILL'S OATH AS REGIDOR OF LOS ANGELES, 1846
Courtesy of Special Collections Library, University of California, Los Angeles.

imposed upon them, California troops under José María Flores revolted against the United States' occupation of Los Angeles and managed to put up a good fight until January of 1847. Andrés Pico, who had succeeded Flores when the latter left for Sonora, was forced to officially surrender the province to John C. Frémont by the Treaty of Cahuenga. One year later, on February 2, 1848, Mexico signed the Treaty of Guadalupe Hidalgo which ended the Mexican War and gave California to the United States.

The change in government did not significantly alter the daily lives of California residents. In fact, it effected a much smaller change than that which would result from some yellow flakes picked up by James Marshall at Sutter's mill a few days earlier. The significance of the discovery of gold on the south fork of the American River on January 24, 1848, could not even be imagined by the unsuspecting citizens of California.

As a result of the Gold Rush of 1849, California had a population large enough to allow its admission to the union in September of 1850. This phenomenal growth, as might be expected, caused a number of changes in the southern portion of the state as well as in the northern center of activity. A new city was now coming into existence in Los Angeles – an American growth grafted upon a Spanish stock. However, because of the inaccessibility of the area, the change from the old order to the new was not as rapid as in other regions. Between Los Angeles and the eastern states was a great gulf of distance and danger, which only the hardiest ventured to cross.

The discovery of gold, which brought some 80,000 people to the northern part of the state in one year, affected the southern part in a reflexive way. In the decade from 1850 to 1860 several thousand of the gold seekers drifted down from San Francisco, some of them with a little capital acquired in the diggings, but more of them penniless; and some of both kinds located permanently in Los Angeles. Also there were those who left the eastern states in the expectation of mining for gold, but were dissuaded by the stories of failure and turned their course to the south, where they were told "men grow rich quickly in raising stock.[8]

But the total number who made their way into this part of the new territory was not large, and of those who came many soon returned to the east, their dreams of sudden wealth failing to materialize. Some commerce was carried on between Los Angeles and Arizona and during the fifties there was trade with the mining camps of the north. The pueblo was a station on the route from Texas and the southern states to the gold fields of northern California, and many of the gold seekers passed through. Except for these sources of revenue, however, the people of Los Angeles enjoyed whatever means that came out of the territory immediately surrounding them.[9]

---

[8] Charles D. Willard, *History of Los Angeles City* (Los Angeles, 1901), 268.

[9] *Ibid.*, 269.

Therefore, during the thirty years from 1850 to 1880, the growth of Los Angeles was slow. It remained throughout most of that period a Spanish-American rather than an American city. The first American census, taken in 1850, showed the population of the city to be 1,610, and of the county 3,530.[10] It has been estimated, however, that prior to the recent gold rush the population in the city had reached almost 3,000. The census of 1860 showed an increase in the city to 4,399 and in the county to 11,333. The next decade resulted in very little population increase, a mere 4,000 in the city and county combined.[11]

The failure to advance was due to the apparent inability of the country to support a larger population. By 1870 the Central and Union Pacific rail connection with the east had been established, but the line was not as yet extended to the southern portion of the state. A regular system of steamers journeyed between Los Angeles and San Francisco, giving the southern city a part of the advantage of the new opening to the east, but still it did not grow. The old Spanish-California tradition of a carefree life, with its interest in music, dancing, fiestas and rodeos, continued through the mid-1870's. By a curious coincidence, the same year bullfighting was abolished (1860), the first baseball club was organized in Los Angeles.[12]

---

[10] Layne, "The First Census," 81-89.

[11] Willard, *History of Los Angeles City*, 270.

[12] Robert G. Cleland, *Cattle on a Thousand Hills* (San Marino, 1951), 83.

In the first period of transition, from 1848 to 1855, many strictly American traditions did, however, come into being. In addition to the laws regarding trial by jury, property rights, and civil authority decreed by the state government, the people of Los Angeles began setting up certain municipal regulations affecting such local matters as schools, newspapers, churches and municipal improvements.

Schools were not entirely unknown during the Mexican regime in Los Angeles, but in the sixty-six years from the founding of the city to the American occupation, there was a total of about ten years of school. These years were scattered along at irregular intervals, the longest stretch of continuous instruction being maintained in a school operated by Don Ignacio Coronel, father of Antonio F. Coronel, from 1838 to 1844. In 1850, after some Americans were elected into the *ayuntamiento,* a school committee was appointed to consider the possibilities of establishing a public school.[13]

William Wolfskill was always a firm believer in education. During the early 1850's he maintained a private school in his home for members of his family and children of neighbors. The curriculum of the school provided a thorough course in English and Spanish as well as instruction in musical education.[14] One of the first teachers Wolfskill employed was

[13] Willard, *History of Los Angeles City,* 272.

[14] Henry D. Barrows, "Pioneer Schools of Los Angeles," in *Annual Publications of the Historical Society of Southern California,* VIII (1909-10), 62.

Rev. J. W. Douglass, founder of *The Pacific,* the first religious newspaper in California. Another teacher was Adolph F. Waldemar, a merchant and civil engineer in Los Angeles during the 1850's. Also employed at the school were a Miss Goodnow and a native Californian who taught Spanish, but by far the most important teacher at the "Old Adobe" was Henry Dwight Barrows.[15]

During a trip north in 1854, William Wolfskill stopped at Benicia to visit his nephew John, who was then attending the Collegiate Institute. On the staff was a young Connecticut "schoolmaster" with a capacity for teaching almost any subject, a talent for playing any musical instrument, and a desire to go to southern California. When Wolfskill offered him a teaching position in his private school, Henry Barrows, "an amiable and reliable scholar of exceptional moral character," [16] accepted with pleasure. Barrows had given up a teaching career in New York to seek his fortune in California gold, and was one of those hardy travelers who had successfully crossed the Isthmus of Panama. Crowded aboard a rickety coast vessel with seventeen hundred other passengers, Barrows finally arrived in the gold fields only to be disappointed by bad luck and to find that he was suffering from malaria contracted on the journey. He began teaching in Benicia in 1852 but thought

---

[15] *Ibid.,* 63.

[16] Richard S. Rust, Principal of Ellington School, Connecticut, letter of reference, Oct. 17, 1842, owned by Henry Barrows' granddaughter Mrs. Thomas Cullen, Los Angeles, California.

the climate further south would be better for his health.[17]

After accepting the job in the middle of November, Barrows went up to the Wolfskill ranch at Río de los Putos to wait until "Uncle Billy" could return to Los Angeles. He helped John and the other boys cut poles and dig holes for a corral fence for the next couple of weeks. When William completed his business at Sacramento, he collected Barrows and his nephew John at the ranch, and the three men headed for San Francisco. Wolfskill booked passage on the steamer "Goliath" and they reached Los Angeles on December 12, 1854. Barrows moved into the "Old Adobe" and began to teach school the next day. From that time forward the young New Englander became closely attached to the Wolfskill family.[18]

Among the students attending Wolfskill's school in December of 1854 were five of William's own children, his nephew John, and Refugio and Francisco Carpenter of Los Nietos.[19] In January of 1855 John Rowland brought his two boys to the school and Wolfskill charged him $25.00 per month tuition for both of them. William (Billy) R. Rowland and another student, Martin G. Aguirre, each served future terms as sheriff of Los Angeles County. In

---

[17] H. D. Barrows, "Diary," Oct. 19, 1854.

[18] *Ibid.*, Dec. 12, 1854; Jan. 20, 1855.

[19] *Ibid.*, Dec. 22, 1854. Lemuel Carpenter had purchased the Santa Gertrudes Rancho from the heirs of Manuel Nieto and established a soap factory on the east bank of the San Gabriel River. Wilson, *History of Los Angeles County,* 35, reports Carpenter as having committed suicide on Nov. 6, 1859 "owing to financial difficulties."

1856 Joseph Edward Pleasants, whose parents were neighbors of John Reid Wolfskill in Solano County, arrived to begin his term at the school and to work on the ranch. Joseph Pleasants described his experience in vivid terms:

> . . . The Wolfskill home was a typical old Californian establishment. The house was a thick walled, low, rambling adobe with a corridor running the entire length of the north and west sides. These were floored with brick and overgrown with vines. There was much activity within these walls and corridors, for besides the family there were a half a dozen of us in the school who lived with the family and another half dozen who came in for the day. Add to this number the numerous working people and we made a small settlement. All, however, was order and harmony . . . each had his own appointed task out of school as well as in, and there was light study or music in the evening.[20]

Pleasants recalled that on the fourth of July of 1856 he was "one of a party of school boys who were, with their teachers, invited to spend a week at the San Fernando Mission." They were guests of Andrés Pico who then occupied the mission as a home. Six boys and a teacher from the public school at Second and Spring attended "and Barrows took Timothy Wolfskill and me." [21]

The first American public school of Los Angeles was authorized by the city council in May of 1854 through the efforts of Stephen C. Foster, one of the

[20] Joseph E. Pleasants, "Los Angeles in 1856," in *Touring Topics*, XXII (January 1930), 37.

[21] Joseph E. Pleasants, "A Fourth of July at San Fernando in 1856," in *Touring Topics*, XXII (February 1930), 49.

early mayors of the city. A graduate of Yale in the class of 1840, Foster succeeded in his attempt to get the school constructed on Spring Street "out of town" where it crossed Second. The school, a one-story brick building, nearly closed after its first term because the city treasury was without funds to maintain it. But William Wolfskill, because of his public spirit and interest in education, came to the rescue and subsidized it.[22] The "Kentucky trapper" generously donated enough money to keep the school going for approximately six months while he continued to maintain his private school.[23]

In January of 1857 occurred a severe earthquake which lasted two full minutes and caused considerable damage. An old man, thrown down in the Plaza, later died of his injuries. Nobody at the Wolfskill school did much that day but talk about the "fearful quake." [24] Joseph Pleasants recalled that

. . . the pruners in the vineyard had just been called to breakfast and were washing their hands at a hydrant, when I noticed them all fall on their knees and begin to pray. I felt dizzy myself, but never having felt an earthquake before did not know what it meant. Everyone was running from the house and crying "temblor."

Billy Rowland told the other students a few days later the shock had been so hard near Fort Tejon that their cattle, which had been grazing on the hills,

---

22 Roy W. Cloud, *Education in California* (Stanford, 1952), 32.

23 Barrows, "Story of an Old Pioneer," in Los Angeles *World,* Oct. 14, 1887.

24 H. D. Barrows, "Diary," Jan. 9, 1857.

lost their footing and fell to the ground. A crack in the earth had opened up for a distance of thirty to forty miles.[25]

It was in the summer of this same year that Henry Barrows made his trip East to pay his respects to President Buchanan and present him with the California wines and fruits. Barrows left San Pedro by steamer for San Francisco and there booked passage on the Pacific Mail Steamship "California." The ship departed on September 5 with four hundred passengers on its regular voyage between San Francisco and Panama.[26] It docked at the Isthmus port on the twenty-third. Barrows took the train to the Atlantic side and the next day boarded the steamer "Star of the West." After a stop-over at Havana and a re-fueling at Key West, the steamer arrived in New York Harbor on October 4, 1857, just one month after Barrows' departure from the northern California port.[27] Travel in 1857 was much improved over the harrowing gold rush days.

William Wolfskill had asked Henry Barrows to purchase a number of books for the school and several other items while in the East. Barrows visited Little, Brown and Company in Boston where he bought the latest twenty-one volume edition of the *Encyclopedia Britannica,* the bound volumes of the *Scientific American,* and other standard reference

[25] Pleasants, "Los Angeles in 1856," 37; Wilson, *History of Los Angeles County,* 53.

[26] H. D. Barrows, "Diary," Sept. 5, 1857; the fare was $283.

[27] *Ibid.,* Oct. 4, 1857.

works. These, together with a Chickering grand
piano, which he had purchased at their factory for
five hundred dollars, and several thousand staves for
wine casks, he had shipped to Los Angeles from
Boston around Cape Horn. Barrows then went down
to Washington to meet President Buchanan and
deliver his gifts.[28]

Wolfskill's head schoolmaster returned to Los Angeles in January of 1858 after having spent an eventful Christmas on board the "Granada" off the coast
of Lower California. According to Barrows' diary of
"12-25 – Christmas," there was a fight among some
soldiers; he had a long talk with a traveler from
Central America; and finally "ate Christmas dinner"
only to find that "one of the colored cooks died of
Panama fever." They held the "burial service in
eve." [29] The ship docked in San Francisco on December 29 and within a week Barrows arrived at the
Wolfskill home to resume his teaching duties. This
might ordinarily have seemed routine to Henry
Barrows after such extensive travels, but by this time
there was an added attraction at the Wolfskill school.
Juana Wolfskill had completed her seventeenth
birthday the previous November and was considered
an exceptionally pretty young lady.[30]

As Joseph Pleasants had noted, life at the Wolfskill
adobe was characterized by simplicity and hospitality. Music and dancing were the principal features
of an evening's entertainment and the Wolfskill girls

28 *Ibid.*, Oct. 5 through 22, 1857.
29 *Ibid.*, Dec. 25, 1857.   30 *Ibid.*, Jan. 7, 1857.

liked to don their velvet dresses and silk embroidered shawls imported from China. There was always singing and until the piano arrived, the principal musical instruments were the harp, violin and guitar.[31] Since Henry Barrows could play them all, he usually ended up in the orchestra. But even so he managed to carry out a courtship of Wolfskill's daughter Juana. They soon became engaged and were married on the 14th of November, 1860. For a wedding present William Wolfskill sent the couple on a three months' journey to the east coast. Henry and Juana Barrows left on the Butterfield Stage from the Bella Union Hotel in December of 1860, and except for a slight delay when the stagecoach turned over at El Monte, rode two thousand miles to Chicago. They spent Christmas at El Paso, where they drank three bottles of El Paso wine, and New Year's Eve in Indian Territory. For Juana, who had never left Los Angeles, it was quite an experience.[32] While they were in Washington, D.C., Henry Barrows received an appointment by President Lincoln as United States Marshal for the Los Angeles district. Barrows performed these duties from 1861 to 1865.[33]

While most of the residents of Los Angeles were discussing the events of the Civil War and the local newspapers were filled with running accounts of the battles, a sad item appeared in the Los Angeles *Star*.

[31] Pleasants, "Los Angeles in 1856," 56.

[32] Juana Wolfskill Barrows, "Diary," Jan. 1, 1861, in private collection of Mrs. Thomas P. Cullen. Henry D. Barrows, "2,000 mile Stage Ride," in *Pico Weekly Chronicle*, Mar. 26, 1909.

[33] Newmark, *Sixty Years in Southern California*, 142.

Magdalena Lugo de Wolfskill had died on the fifth of July, 1862, at the age of fifty-eight. The funeral was held at the Plaza Church and attended by many of the Wolfskill friends.[34] Just six months later Juana Wolfskill Barrows became gravely ill and died in the arms of her husband on January 31, 1863.[35] Another funeral was held at the Plaza Church.

In addition to the normal pursuit of his career in agriculture and his firm support of education, William Wolfskill had several other interests. His early experience as a trader was not forgotten and he had much more than a mountain man's acquaintance with the economic activities of California. Wolfskill was a wise businessman and a successful land speculator. His ledger book contained the accounts of many pueblo citizens and some of the most prominent people in Los Angeles owed him money. During the late 1840's and 1850's Wolfskill lent money to such well-known names as Pico, Castro, Sepulveda, Bandini, Stearns, Carrillo, Lugo, Sutter, Ximeno, Vallejo, Yorba, Olivera, Alvarado, Figueroa, Reid, Mellus, Sainsevain and Limantour. Usually the amounts ran from as little as three hundred dollars to as much as ten thousand dollars, with interest at the rate of 1% to 2% per month.[36] At his death in 1866 Wolfskill

34 "Obituary," Los Angeles *Star,* July 10, 1862. The funeral announcement can be found in the Lewis Wolfskill Papers, Huntington Library.

35 H. D. Barrows, "Diary," Jan. 31, 1863; Juana Wolfskill was apparently suffering from tuberculosis.

36 William Wolfskill, "Ledger II, 1843 to 1854," Film no. 222, Huntington Library.

held more than fifteen thousand dollars in notes from various citizens.[37]

In 1855 Don José Sepulveda and his wife, Francisca, borrowed $10,000 from Wolfskill. This note was secured by a mortgage on the Rancho San Joaquin, consisting of "eleven square leagues of land, more or less," near present day Laguna Beach, and ran for one year. It called for monthly interest payments of two percent. The note was paid off when due and netted Wolfskill $2,400.[38]

Wolfskill also did considerable business with the missions in California and his account book included those at San Luis Obispo, Santa Barbara, San Jose, San Gabriel and Mission Dolores.[39] During 1863 and 1864 Benito D. Wilson borrowed a total of $3,400 with interest at 2% per month and in 1866 Abel Stearns borrowed $2,445.51 with interest at the "low" rate of only 1% per month. Wolfskill was, however, generous with relatives, as his son-in-law Henry Barrows received almost $4,000 in loans with no interest.[40]

In 1860 William Wolfskill purchased Rancho Lomas de Santiago from Don Teodosio Yorba and his wife Doña Inocencia Reyes de Yorba for $7,000. The rancho was "bounded on the North by the Santa

[37] Inventory of Property in Los Angeles County, *Estate of William Wolfskill, Deceased,* Case no. 313, filed Oct. 29, 1866. Records of the Superior Court of the State of California, Los Angeles County.

[38] Robert G. Cleland, *The Irvine Ranch of Orange County* (San Marino, 1962), 49.

[39] Wolfskill, "Ledger II, 1843 to 1854."

[40] Inventory of Property, *Estate of William Wolfskill.*

Ana River, East by the mountains, South by Rancho Aliso, and west by the Rancho San Joaquin." [41] The boundary of this rancho was subsequently the subject of much controversy and it was finally shown that the entire grant was unlawfully made by Governor Pico and was nullified by the Treaty of Guadalupe Hidalgo. The U.S. Land Commission, however, confirmed the grant to Yorba in 1854 and a patent was issued in 1868 for eleven square leagues, or 47,226.16 acres, as the amount of land contained within the rancho.[42]

Soon after the acquisition of Lomas de Santiago, Wolfskill brought down carpenters and lumber from Los Angeles and proceeded to construct a house on the bank of the Santiago Creek. When the house was only about half finished he became involved with the Yorbas, who still owned the adjoining rancho of Santiago de Santa Ana, on the question of the boundary. The late Terry E. Stephenson, a pioneer of Santa Ana and writer of Orange County history, described the incident as follows:

> The house was no more than half-finished when two of the Yorbas rode up on horseback and courteously informed Mr. Wolfskill that he was building his house on the Rancho Santiago de Santa Ana, which belonged to the Yorba and Peralta heirs and which had not yet been partitioned.
>
> The contention of the Yorbas proved to be correct. The situation, however, was quickly remedied by the resourceful Mr. Wolfskill. He looked up two or three of the several

---

41 Los Angeles County, *Book of Deeds*, v, p. 203.

42 *Mexican Land Grant Frauds*, Hearings before the Senate Committee on Public Lands and Surveys, 69 Cong., 2 sess. (Washington, 1927), p. 73.

scores of heirs and bought their interests in the old rancho. That gave him as much right to be on the Rancho Santiago de Santa Ana as anyone else had, and throughout the six years that Mr. Wolfskill owned the Rancho Lomas de Santiago, his stock had the freedom of the hills as far north as the Santa Ana River, just as that freedom seems to have been accorded to others who were heirs or who had acquired an interest in the historic old Spanish land grant.[43]

Wolfskill purchased Lomas de Santiago for the purpose of grazing his recently acquired stock of cattle. He placed Joseph Pleasants, who had been residing and working at the Wolfskill home for the previous four years, in charge of the ranch as foreman.[44] During the 1850's cattle prices were high because of the demand created by the gold rush. At one time in this period John Reid Wolfskill sold a thousand head of cattle from his ranch for $40,000 cash.[45] During the 'sixties, however, overproduction followed by a disasterous drought forced prices downward.

In the area surrounding Los Angeles many cattle ranchers were faced with the problem of rustlers. The Los Angeles *Star* contained frequent accounts of their activities and referred particularly to the losses sustained by William Wolfskill, Abel Stearns and Benito D. Wilson, who were three of the largest landowners. The general rumor was that the outlaws had

[43] Terry E. Stephenson, *In the Shadows of Old Saddleback* (Santa Ana, Calif., 1931), 46.

[44] Samuel Armor, *The History of Orange County, California* (Los Angeles, 1911), 113.

[45] Barrows, "Story of an Old Pioneer," in Los Angeles *World*, Oct. 14, 1887.

a rendezvous on the Mojave River, from which the stolen stock was driven to Salt Lake City and other Mormon settlements or towns for sale.[46] In the summer of 1862 a nephew of Wolfskill's encountered a band of rustlers rounding up his uncle's cattle. The youth fought a running battle with them until both he and his horse were wounded. The thieves were then able to successfully drive off the Wolfskill herd, as well as adding to it the herd from Rancho Los Coyotes.[47]

Cattle prices, which had declined seriously in the fall of 1862 because of the drought, dropped lower and lower as the drought continued. In January of 1863, Abel Stearns reluctantly agreed to sell a thousand of his best cattle to Miller and Lux of San Francisco for eight dollars a head; a few months later multitudes of starving animals were being slaughtered for the trifling value of their hides and horns.[48] To make matters worse, the late spring brought a succession of hard, scorching winds from the desert, and millions of grasshoppers devastated the country. A few rancheros were fortunate enough to find pasturage in the mountains for portions of their herds, but many lost up to seventy-five percent of their stock. Joseph Pleasants recalled that

[46] Los Angeles *Star,* Sept. 28, 1861. As early as Feb. 14, 1852, the *Star* reported that Wolfskill and Michael White had lost between three and four thousand sheep supposedly driven off by Colorado Indians to the Mojave Desert.

[47] C. R. Johnson to Abel Stearns, July 24, 1862.   Stearns Papers, Huntington Library.

[48] Cleland, *Cattle on a Thousand Hills,* 175.

Now on this Day Comes

William Wolfskill

and tenders the ~ Mark ~ in the margin as the ~ Mark ~ assumed by him ~; And having examined the Record of Marks, Brands and Counter Brands, and feeling satisfied that it is unlike any in the County, and as far as my knowledge extends, different from any in the State; I therefore record it as the Lawful ~ Mark ~ of the said William Wolfskill ~

this 15th day of ~ May ~ 1861

John W. Shore Recorder.

~~Deputy~~

STATE OF CALIFORNIA,
COUNTY OF LOS ANGELES.
} ss.   COUNTY RECORDER'S OFFICE.

I, John W. Shore, County Clerk of the County Court of Los Angeles County, State of California, and Ex-Officio County Recorder, Hereby Certify, That the above and foregoing is a full, true and correct copy of the original, as the same appears of record in my Office.

In Witness Whereof, I have hereunto set my hand and affixed my Official seal this the 29th day of ~ May ~ A. D. 1861

John W. Shore Recorder.

~~Deputy~~

EAR-MARK BRAND OF WILLIAM WOLFSKILL, 1861
Courtesy of John C. Wolfskill.

. . . not over four inches of rain fell . . . from October 1863 to June 1864. The Southeast wind would start with every favorable indication of rain. It would cloud up and all the rancheros would begin to rejoice in the prospect, when the desert or so-called "Santa Ana" wind would set in and scatter every cloud on the horizon. The wind would blow for days, parching the already dry ground and shattering the hopes of the stock men. The stock were getting thin and something had to be done if they were to be saved.[49]

In the summer of 1863 William Wolfskill had gone out to Tonopah to look after some mining interests which he had purchased in San Bernardino County. While traveling down the Mojave River he noticed that the bottom lands were covered with grass for a distance of some twenty or thirty miles along the river's course. He decided that if the drought continued he would transfer his stock to this subirrigated pasturage east of the San Bernardino Mountains. When mid-winter arrived and still no rain fell, Wolfskill prepared to move his stock. He told his friends John Rowland and William Workman, owners of Rancho La Puente, about the grassy bottom lands and invited them to join him. Joseph Pleasants and his former classmate Billy Rowland took charge of their respective herds, which totaled over five thousand head of cattle and almost one thousand horses,[50] and started moving out in early January.

[49] Joseph E. Pleasants, "Ranging on the Mojave River in 1864," in *Touring Topics*, XXII (March 1930), 42.

[50] Wolfskill had about two thousand head of cattle and three hundred horses.

. . . We took about 500 head at a drive, going slowly and feeding them along the road where it was possible. It took about six vaqueros to the bunch and a teamster with a wagon and the camp outfit. We averaged only about fifteen miles a day as the stock were thin and the feed poor. At San Bernardino where Mr. Wolfskill owned some land, we laid by a few days and rested up the stock before crossing the mountains. We went out through the Cajon Pass, over the summit and across the desert to the Mojave River.

The going was rough at times because of sleet storms and very cold winds blowing through the pass. The vaqueros even found icicles hanging from their horses' bridle bits. By the end of March, 1864, Joseph Pleasants and Billy Rowland were well settled on the Mojave. They remained on the desert for more than a year and the cattle were provided with sufficient feed. Even though it began to rain on November 16, 1864, and continued at intervals through the following winter, they did not begin to move the cattle home until April of 1865. The last drive was completed by the middle of May. Wolfskill and the La Puente ranchers lost only about twenty-five percent of their stock, a much smaller loss than that sustained by those who did not move their herds. The Yorbas and some other owners drove cattle far below the border into Lower California but were not as fortunate.[51] The southern counties' cattle industry never really recovered from the "terrible year of 1864."[52]

[51] C. R. Johnson to Abel Stearns, June 1, 2, 13, 1863.   Stearns Papers, Huntington Library.

[52] Pleasants, "Ranging on the Mojave River," 43.

In 1866 Wolfskill sold Rancho Lomas de Santiago and his share in Rancho Santiago de Santa Ana to a group of pioneer sheepmen from Monterey County. Jotham, Llewelyn, and Marcellus Bixby; Dr. Thomas and Benjamin Flint; and James Irvine had made large profits from the demand for wool caused by the disruption of the cotton industry during the Civil War. By the mid-sixties they had decided to extend their operations to southern California and began the systematic purchase of several of the largest ranchos in Los Angeles County. They paid Wolfskill $7,000 for his property, the same price he had paid the Yorbas six years before.[53] This change of ownership came just as the court commissioners were dividing up the old Rancho Santiago de Santa Ana. In the final adjustment, James Irvine and his partners, Flint, Bixby and Company, were allotted a strip of land a mile wide running the full length of the southeast line of the rancho. This was in settlement of their rights as purchasers from Wolfskill of the rights secured by him in 1860.[54] Irvine eventually bought out his partners interests, which also included Rancho San Joaquin purchased from the Sepulvedas, and in 1876 became owner of approximately one hundred thousand acres in present Orange County.[55]

As a result of the drought in the early sixties, Wolfskill held a mortgage on Andrés Duarte's Rancho Azusa, which consisted of one and one-half

[53] Los Angeles County, *Book of Deeds,* VII, pp. 604-06.
[54] Stephenson, *In the Shadows of Old Saddleback,* 46.
[55] Los Angeles County, *Book of Deeds,* XLVIII, p. 436.

square leagues or about 6,500 acres in the San Gabriel Valley. Wolfskill was forced to foreclose on the land in December of 1863 and was awarded the ranch for his own bid of four thousand dollars at the sheriff's sale. Rancho Azusa, situated just north of Rancho Santa Anita, was sold in 1868 by Wolfskill's son Luis to Alexander Weill, a New York capitalist. Weill and Wolfskill had taken the first steps to develop water for the mutual benefit of the ranches.[56]

In 1865 William Wolfskill also bought Rancho Santa Anita, which had formerly belonged to the "Scotch Paisano" Hugo Reid. The ranch had passed through the ownership of Henry Dalton, who raised wheat for use in his own flour mill; Joseph A. Rowe, the circus man; and finally to the land company of Corbitt, Dibblee and Barker.[57] At the time of purchase, Wolfskill paid $20,000 for an area of land containing between nine and ten thousand acres. This rancho was "bounded on the north by public lands, west by lands belonging to L. J. Rose, south by public lands, and east by Azusa Rancho." Even then Rancho Santa Anita was a productive agricultural unit.[58] Wolfskill experimented in the raising of eucalyptus trees from seeds sent to him by a friend in Australia and was one of the first to grow a tree of this kind in California.[59] Wolfskill bequeathed this property to his son Luis, who would later marry Henry Dalton's

[56] W. W. Robinson, *Ranchos Become Cities* (Pasadena, 1939), 193.

[57] *Ibid.*, 192.

[58] Inventory of Property, *Estate of William Wolfskill.*

[59] William A. Spaulding, *History and Reminiscences of Los Angeles City and County, California* (Los Angeles, n.d.), 204.

daughter Luisa. Luis Wolfskill worked the ranch until he was made a good offer. Harris Newmark recalled that

> . . . It was in March (1872) that we purchased . . . the Santa Anita rancho . . . paying eighty-five thousand dollars for this beautiful domain. The terms agreed upon were twenty thousand dollars down and four equal quarterly payments for the balance. In light of the aftermath [another severe drought] the statement that our expectations of prospective wool profits inspired this purchase seem ludicrous, but it was far from laughable at the time. . .[60]

Lucky Baldwin paid $200,000 for the same property in 1875.[61]

Wolfskill acquired title to a portion of Rancho San Francisco, the site of present-day Newhall, through an effort to assist his friend Ignacio del Valle. Believing that the depression in cattle prices was temporary, del Valle's stepmother, Jacoba Felix de Salazar began to borrow heavily on the rancho. Wolfskill held a mortgage of $8,500 and those held by others amounted to another $8,000.[62] In the face of threatened foreclosure, Ignacio del Valle asked Wolfskill to pay off all creditors and assume the entire debt of $16,350. The two men then worked out an agreement by which Wolfskill filed a demand for foreclosure and purchased the ranch at the ensuing sheriff's sale for the $16,350 owed to him.[63] He then

---

[60] Newmark, *Sixty Years in Southern California*, 439.

[61] Robinson, *Ranchos Become Cities*, 192.

[62] Ruth Waldo Newhall, *The Newhall Ranch* (San Marino, 1958), 44.

[63] Agreement between William Wolfskill and Ygnacio del Valle, April 28, 1864. Del Valle Collection, Los Angeles County Museum.

deeded five-elevenths of the property to Ignacio del
Valle. By this device the Salazars no longer had any
interest in the ranch and Ignacio was free of the
burden of his stepmother's debts.

The drought of 1863-64 had left the del Valles,
as well as many other California families, in tight
circumstances, but the discovery of a new fuel –
petroleum – was to put them back in the credit column. It was found that the most promising oil territory lay in the valley of the Santa Clara River and
that the Rancho San Francisco appeared to have the
greatest possibilities. Thomas Bard, nephew of the
president of the Pennsylvania Railroad Co., approached Wolfskill and Ignacio del Valle to discuss
the prospects of purchasing the land. On March 18,
1865, the owners agreed to sell the ranch to Bard for
$53,320, out of which William Wolfskill received
$21,307. Bard then sold to Ignacio del Valle, as part
of the agreement, thirteen hundred acres surrounding his Camulos ranchhouse for five hundred dollars.
Rancho San Francisco was promptly deeded to the
Philadelphia and California Petroleum Company.
Thomas Bard became not only an important figure
in the California oil industry, but later a United
States senator.[64]

The Los Angeles *Tri-Weekly News* gave a list of
the incomes of those citizens in the city and county
paying federal income taxes for the year 1864. Richard Savage, United States Assessor for the Second

---

[64] Newhall, *Newhall Ranch,* 47.

District of California, listed the income of William Wolfskill, the second highest, at $7,215. The man with the largest income was Phineas Banning with $20,000. Included among the one hundred twelve names were J. M. Griffith, $5,000; J. Tomlinson, $5,000; J. L. Sainsevain, $2,000; Charles Ducommun, $684; Manuel Requena, $181; and F. P. Ramirez, $14. This news item was accompanied by the tongue-in-cheek comment that

> . . . It appears to us if one had a small capital to invest he could make money by buying (provided the poor man would sell) the incomes of some of the above at the figures given to the assessor. We believe the business would pay a good interest on the money invested.[65]

William Wolfskill had always been somewhat apprehensive about spending money for the construction of commercial buildings in the city of Los Angeles. In 1858 he had set up his son Timothy in the dry goods business in partnership with Solomon Lazard,[66] but had not invested on a large scale. In December of 1860, as he passed the Temple Block on his way back from the funeral of Henry Mellus, Wolfskill is quoted as having remarked: "What a pity! If Temple had not built so much he might now be a rich man!"[67] But the firm of Lazard and Wolf-

---

[65] Los Angeles *Tri-Weekly News*, Mar. 25, 1865.

[66] Solomon Lazard, a native of Lorraine, arrived in California in 1851 and associated with his cousin Maurice Kremer under the title of Lazard & Kremer in Los Angeles in 1853. Timothy Wolfskill assumed Kremer's interest in the partnership.

[67] Warner, *Historical Sketch of Los Angeles County*, 118.

skill prospered, albeit without the help of Timothy who had gone to Mexico,[68] and William decided to invest in a larger store. When John Temple died in May of 1866 (leaving an estate worth one-half million dollars), William Wolfskill purchased a block of property on Main Street from the executors. The following announcement appeared in the Los Angeles *Semi-Weekly News:*

> William Wolfskill, Esq., of this city, has commenced grading a lot on Main Street, adjoining the Lafayette Hotel, for the erection of a new store to be occupied by Messrs. S. Lazard & Co., as a dry goods store. The store will be 50 feet front and 96 feet deep, two stories high, of brick, fireproof, and will be when completed one of the largest, most substantial buildings south of San Francisco. One by one the old adobe buildings, the relics of a former and more incomplete age of civilization are giving way to a more useful and ornamental class of building.[69]

Wolfskill invested twenty thousand dollars in the store, which would be operated by Solomon Lazard, but did not live to see it finished. Construction of the new dry goods emporium was completed during the administration of his estate.[70]

During the 1860's William Wolfskill strongly supported the Union cause in the War between the States. He was a candidate for Public Administrator

---

[68] H. D. Barrows, "Diary," Dec. 13, 1858; Jan. 1, 1859. Timothy had gone to work in the "Gila Mines" and did not return to Los Angeles.

[69] Los Angeles *Semi-Weekly News,* May 1, 1866.

[70] Inventory and Appraisement, *Estate of William Wolfskill.* At the time of Wolfskill's death, S. Lazard & Co. was holding $9,152.17 in cash which had been advanced by Wolfskill.

of Los Angeles County on the Republican supported People's Union County Ticket in 1860, and was eventually elected to that office in September of 1865.[71] Wolfskill served on numerous civic committees during this period and was particularly concerned with the development of transportation and communication in the southern portion of the state. His term as Public Administrator was interrupted by his death in 1866.

[71] Los Angeles *Tri-Weekly News*, Sept. 19, 1865.

8

Pioneer Legacy

> *O to die advancing on!*
> *Are there some of us to droop and die?*
> > > > *has the hour come?*
> *Then upon the march we fittest die,*
> > > *soon and sure the gap is fill'd*
> > *Pioneers! O pioneers!*
> > > > > – Walt Whitman

The summer of 1866 was a pleasant one in Los Angeles. There had been sufficient rainfall during the previous spring to provide the foothills with a covering of new grass, and the vineyards and orchards had yielded an excellent crop. All should have been well at the "Old Adobe," but William Wolfskill's health was failing. He continued to work around the ranch, experimenting with his recently purchased gang-plow, a new tool containing a machine for sowing seed and a harrow, but was forced to let his son Joseph take sole charge of the agricultural activities. It had also become difficult for him to carry out his responsibilities as Public Administrator and to supervise his wide variety of business interests.

On September 16, 1866, Wolfskill had a slight heart attack which sent him to bed. His feet became swollen and it was impossible for the old trapper to walk. Joseph and his sisters, Francisca and Magdalena, kept a constant vigil and Luis was called in from

Rancho Santa Anita. He began to improve and a few days later was feeling well enough to think seriously about organizing his affairs. On September 20, Wolfskill decided to draw up his Last Will and Testament. He wanted his brother Mathus, his son Joseph, and his good friend Henry Barrows to act as the executors of his estate in the event of his death.[1]

The most valuable piece of property which William Wolfskill owned was the Los Angeles site of his large adobe residence and his first orchard and vineyard. The legal description of his "home property" was as follows:

A certain tract of land situated in Los Angeles City, Los Angeles County, State of California, bounded and described as follows, to wit: On the East by Alameda Street; on the West by San Pedro or Foster St. and land of A. Briswalter and others; on the South by land of A. F. Coronel, by Kohler's vineyard, by Weibels garden and other lands; on the North by land of E. Vaché, W. Woodworth and others – said tract of land containing about 70 acres. With vineyard, orchard, orange groves, walnut grove and other improvements, including houses, barns &c &c

Val'd at $25,000.00 [2]

Wolfskill bequeathed one half of this property, "including the dwelling house and other improvements," to his son Joseph, and the other half, which included the "Casildo Aguilar vineyard, Bernacio Sotello vineyard, the Brundige vineyard, the Ramón Valenzuela vineyard and the land purchased from Lewis

---

[1] H. D. Barrows, "Diary," Sept. 20, 1866.
[2] Inventory and Appraisement, *Estate of William Wolfskill.*

Lamonary" to his daughter Francisca Wolfskill Shephard.[3] It was out of this property that Joseph Wolfskill gave fourteen acres to the Southern Pacific Railroad in order to bring its services to the city. When this land was eventually subdivided in the 1890's, it became known as the Wolfskill Orchard Tract.[4]

To his daughter Magdalena Wolfskill Sabichi, Wolfskill bequeathed a vineyard on the east side of the Los Angeles River "containing about 60 acres, more or less, bounded North by land of E. Moulton and others; East by Mariana Ruiz and others; West by the Los Angeles River and on the South by land that formerly belonged to L. Rose"; it was appraised at six thousand dollars.[5] He also wanted his youngest daughter to have the thirty acre "Mullally Vineyard" bounded by the property of Juan Sepulveda, John Dorn, Loma Street and "a Cross Street"; a store on Main Street "known as Apothecaries' Hall"; and a house and lot above the Catholic Church.[6]

To his granddaughter, Alice Barrows, only child of Juana and Henry Barrows, Wolfskill bequeathed the "Scott Vineyard" located in the southern part of the city. It contained "about 70 acres of land, more or less," and was valued at six thousand dollars. The lands of J. A. Watson lay to the north, Alameda

---

[3] "Will of Wm. Wolfskill, Esq.," in Los Angeles *Semi-Weekly News,* Oct. 9, 1866.

[4] Newmark, *Sixty Years in Southern California,* 357.

[5] Inventory and Appraisement, *Estate of William Wolfskill.*

[6] "Will of Wm. Wolfskill, Esq.," *loc. cit.*

Street to the west, the Los Angeles River to the east and land "supposed to belong to J. L. Sainsevain" to the south. A number of improvements had been made on this land.[7] Wolfskill also left Alice five thousand dollars in gold coin, store property on Los Angeles Street, the mortgages due on several pieces of property, casks for 12,000 gallons of wine, ten fermenting tubs, a Chickering piano and an Estey organ. All of this property was to be held in trust by Henry Barrows until his daughter, then only five years old, would reach her majority.[8]

Luis Wolfskill was to receive the Azusa Rancho, valued at three thousand dollars; Rancho Santa Anita, "bounded North . . . and South by public land; West by lands that belong to L. J. Rose; and East by Azusa Rancho, containing 8,000 acres more or less, valued at $15,000";[9] and an eight-day clock.[10]

To his two grandchildren, William and Leonora Cardwell, Wolfskill decided to leave a house and some property in San Bernardino. Wolfskill owned approximately forty lots in that city, worth a total of about four thousand dollars,[11] which he had purchased following the U.S. Government Survey of

---

7 Inventory and Appraisement, *Estate of William Wolfskill.*

8 Petition of Henry D. Barrows to the Superior Court of Los Angeles County for release from guardianship of daughter Alice Wolfskill Barrows, Sept. 30, 1880. Ms, Alice Wolfskill Barrows Papers, Special Collections Library, University of California, Los Angeles.

9 Inventory and Appraisement, *Estate of William Wolfskill.*

10 "Will of Wm. Wolfskill, Esq.," *loc. cit.*

11 Inventory and Appraisement, *Estate of William Wolfskill.*

1860. Wolfskill also left the Cardwells a store on Main Street in Los Angeles occupied by William Buffum, Esq. To Joseph, Francisca and Magdalena Wolfskill, he bequeathed the store then being constructed on Main Street for S. Lazard & Co. and "the mill property in San Bernardino." [12]

Wolfskill wanted his personal property, valued at nearly fifty thousand dollars, to be divided equally among all of his children. He had acquired an impressive number of items during his thirty-five year residency in California and always took pride in the excellent library and fine furnishings of his Los Angeles home. The silverware alone was worth one hundred dollars. Other valuable personal belongings included two pianos, various farm implements, and the wine-making equipment. Among the livestock listed in his property inventory were two mules worth $250; five jackasses, one worth $500 and four worth $50 each; 2,343 sheep valued at $1.50 a head or $3,514.50; 204 mares valued at $2,040; and 214 head of horned cattle worth about $1,500. In addition, his personal property included a one-fourth interest in a "Quartz Mining Mill and Mine" in Kern County, about ten thousand dollars in cash on hand, and another twenty-five thousand dollars due from promissory notes and personal loans.[13]

A conservative estimate of the value of all of Wolfskill's property, both real and personal, is a

<hr>

12 "Will of Wm. Wolfskill, Esq.," *loc. cit.*
13 Inventory and Appraisement, *Estate of William Wolfskill.*

figure somewhere in the neighborhood of one hundred fifty thousand dollars. This amount, based on the value of ranch property and standard of living in 1866, is a considerable fortune to have been made by a man who arrived in California in 1831 "without means or resources and heavy debts in New Mexico." [14]

A few days after Wolfskill had completed the drawing up of his will and the settling of his other affairs, he was approached by Henry Barrows on the subject of having his picture taken. Since there were no pictures of him in existence, Barrows insisted it should be done right away. Wolfskill finally consented and Barrows hurried off to get Henry Penelon, a talented local artist and photographer. On September 27, 1866, Penelon came to the house and prepared to take the picture while Barrows and his friend Eugene Meyer carried Wolfskill out onto the north corridor.[15] The task was quickly completed and fortunately the picture turned out well, because six days later, on October 3, William Wolfskill was dead. The heart trouble from which he had suffered for many years had eventually caused his death at the age of sixty-eight years and six months. Henry Barrows made the following comment in his diary:

Mr. W. died at 8½ A.M. after a long and useful life – work done and well done. He has found rest! He was indeed a good man. Funeral tomorrow. He was like a father to me.

14 Barrows, "William Wolfskill, the Pioneer," 295.
15 H. D. Barrows, "Diary," Sept. 27, 1866.

THE ONLY KNOWN PHOTOGRAPH OF WILLIAM WOLFSKILL
Taken by Henri Penelon, Los Angeles, September 27, 1866.
Courtesy of John C. Wolfskill.

The funeral was held on October 4, 1866 at the Plaza Church in Los Angeles. There was a long procession and Father Francisco Mora, later bishop of the diocese, said a High Mass. The priest, who had long been a friend of the Wolfskill family, spoke at the grave in Spanish and sadly reflected the sentiments of all those attending.[16] According to his fellow citizens, Wolfskill "was truly one of the pioneers of California, who for more than a quarter of a century had watched with zealous eye the fortunes of his adopted state." He "was able to say he had seen the desert blossom as the rose. When he arrived in this place, the thousands of acres that are now covered with vines loaded with delicious grapes were then but a sandy desert." [17] William Wolfskill had witnessed a great many changes in Los Angeles and had contributed significantly to their positive effect on the growth and development of southern California. Despite the limited scope of his formal education, Wolfskill was a man of intelligence and extreme resourcefulness.

Perhaps as the result of his many activities, Wolfskill had little time for writing. All that exist today from his own hand are a few business letters and his account books. That he wrote fluent Spanish is evidenced by a letter to Antonio María Lugo regarding a cattle transaction with Abel Stearns.[18] If he kept a

[16] *Ibid.,* Oct. 3-4, 1866.

[17] "Died . . . Mr. William Wolfskill," in Los Angeles *Semi-Weekly News,* Oct. 5, 1866.

[18] Guillermo Wolfskill to Antonio María Lugo, July 3, 1843. Stearns Papers, Huntington Library.

diary, it has not been discovered, and he passed away before Hubert Howe Bancroft began compiling information for his "Pioneer Register and Index." Because of these facts, it is difficult to determine Wolfskill's personal feelings on various matters. It is possible, however, to gain an insight into the character of this early California pioneer through the writings of his contemporaries and early California historians.

Bancroft stated that William Wolfskill "approved of the principles of vigilance but he would never have consented to take any active part in their transactions. He was a very modest, retiring man and could not endure being put in a conspicuous position." [19] Harris Newmark commented that ". . . despite the disappointments of his more eventful years, he was a man of marked intelligence and remained unembittered and kindly disposed toward his fellow men." [20] Major Horace Bell, one of the early rangers in California, thought William Wolfskill was truly representative of the pioneer spirit. Bell wrote:

> The first few days after my arrival in Los Angeles, I visited the then famous vineyard of William Wolfskill, the best then in California. Mr. Wolfskill was a very remarkable man; in fact, he was a hero – not the kind of a hero poets like to sing about, but still a hero. A man of indomitable will, industry and self-denial; an American pioneer hero; one who

---

[19] Bancroft, H. H., "A sketch of the Active Part Taken in the Historical Development of California by . . . William Wolfskill." Ms, Bancroft Library.

[20] Newmark, *Sixty Years in Southern California,* 357.

succeeds in all he undertakes, and is always to be trusted, of the kind of men who enrich the country in which they live. . .[21]

In a brief biographical sketch written fifty years after Wolfskill's death, Nellie Van de Grift Sanchez concluded that Wolfskill was "a man of alert and receptive mentality," and was known for his "extensive reading, his mature judgment and his sterling personal characteristics." Wolfskill's life "was moulded in a stern school of experience and he placed true value upon his fellow men." Finally, he was "true and loyal in all that makes for noble manhood, and his name merits high place on the role of honored pioneers of California." [22]

Of those who have passed judgment on the person of William Wolfskill, the writer who probably knew him best was Henry Dwight Barrows. Having lived with the Wolfskill family for eight years prior to his marriage to Wolfskill's daughter, Barrows had a good opportunity to observe "Mr. W" in a variety of situations. Barrows was constantly amazed at the strong physical constitution and immense amount of vital energy which Wolfskill possessed, and thought that the ex-mountain man could accomplish anything he set his mind to.[23] Barrows was also impressed that Wolfskill was one of the few Americans or foreigners in California who always dealt fairly and honestly with the native Californians. As a result, "Don

[21] Major Horace Bell, *Reminiscences of a Ranger* (Santa Barbara, 1927), 58.
[22] Sanchez, *California and Californians*, III, p. 117.
[23] Barrows, "William Wolfskill, the Pioneer," 297.

Guillermo" was almost worshipped by the earlier generation of "hijos del país" who spoke only the Spanish language and who, therefore, needed impartial and disinterested advice on many important matters. "The admiration, even veneration, for Mr. Wolfskill was unbounded."[24]

Henry Barrows believed that Wolfskill exhibited in all things the prime human qualities of honesty, sincerity and simplicity. In addition he had one quality that "was as rare as it was admirable." It seemed to have become second nature to Wolfskill "to construe charitably the motives of everybody, friends and foes alike. When others riled at the acts or words of their neighbors, he would always seek to suggest a charitable motive for their conduct. Apparently he had originally adopted this rule of universal charity from principle, and finally practiced it from the spontaneous promptings of a naturally kind heart."[25]

In religion Wolfskill believed in the teachings of the Bible, and at his death received the final blessings of the Roman Catholic Church.[26] William Wolfskill – trapper, trader, ranchero and citizen of two countries – was truly a member of that indefinable body of men who believe that a loyal and understanding heart and a good life are the best preparations for death.

---

[24] Henry D. Barrows, "The Story of a Native Californian [Ramón Valenzuela]," in *Annual Publications of the Historical Society of Southern California,* IV (1898), 117.

[25] Barrows, "William Wolfskill, the Pioneer," 297.

[26] H. D. Barrows, "Diary," Oct. 3, 1866.

Appendix

Inventories and Appraisements of Property
in the Estate of William Wolfskill
in the Counties of
Los Angeles and San Bernardino

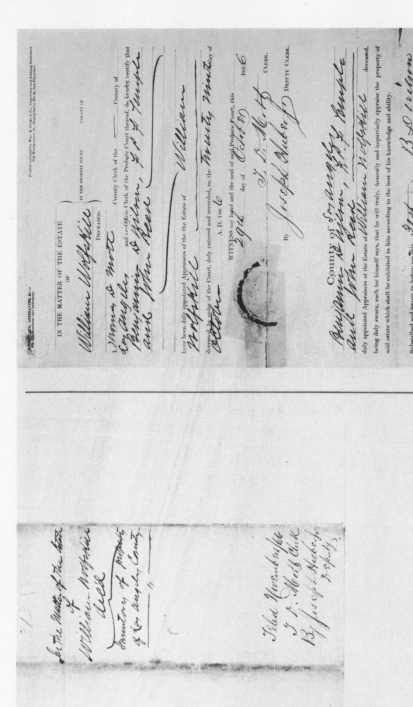

IN THE MATTER OF THE ESTATE

OF

William Wolfskill

DECEASED.

IN THE PROBATE COURT

COUNTY OF

County of _____

I, _____ County Clerk of the _____ County of _____ and ex-Officio Clerk of the Probate Court thereof, do hereby verify that Benjamin D. Wilson, F. P. F. Temple and John Reese _____ William _____

have been duly appointed Appraisers of the the Estate of _____ William Wolfskill deceased, by order of the Court, duly entered and recorded, on the Twenty Ninth day of _____ A. D. 186 6

WITNESS my hand and the seal of said Probate Court, this 29th day of Oct 1866

J. L. Mott CLERK.

By Joseph Huber DEPUTY CLERK.

County of Los Angeles

Benjamin D. Wilson, F. P. F. Temple and John Reese

duly appointed Appraisers of the Estate of William Wolfskill deceased, being duly sworn, each for himself says, that he will truly, honestly and impartially appraise the property of said estate which shall be exhibited to him according to the best of his knowledge and ability.

B. D. Wilson
F. P. F. Temple
John Reese

Subscribed and sworn to before me This 31st day of October A. D. 186

J. L. Mott Clerk
By Joseph Huber Dpty

In The Matter of The Estate
of
William Wolfskill
deceased
Inventory of Property
of Los Angeles County

Filed November 5th 1866
J. L. Mott Clerk
By Joseph Huber Dpty

List of the Real and Personal Property
belonging to the Estate of William Wolfskill
deceased —

Real Property:

1. A certain Tract of land situated in
Los Angeles City, Los Angeles County, State
of California, bounded and situated
as follows, to wit: On the East by Alameda
Street; On the North by San Pedro or Main
St and lands of A Pridham and others;
On the South by land of L R O'Connor, by
Mohler's Vineyard by Nichols garden —
on the land; On the North by land of
B Yarbé, W Woodworth & others — this
Tract containing about 4 acres
of Vines. With Vineyard, orange grove,
orange grove, orchard, pump deck and
other improvements in excellent
houses Vines &c &c
Val'd at $ 25,000.00

2. A Vineyard in the Section or part of the City
of Los Angeles, County of Los Angeles, State of
California, and known as the "____"
Vineyard Containing about 70 acres
of land, more or less, bounded North
by land of J R Mathews; On the West
by Alameda St.; On the East by

On Angeles Rivulet on the South
by land supposed to belong to
Mr Saiserain —
       Val'd at $ 6,000.00

3. A body of land and Vineyard
situated on the East side of Los
Angeles River Containing about
60– acres, more or less, bounded
North by land of E Merinta
and others; East by a Vineyard a
Vineyard and others; West by the
Los Angeles River; and on the South
by land that formed & belonged
to ____ now deceased. —this
body of land situate in Los Angeles
City County State   Val'd at $ 6,000.00

4. A Vineyard situated in Los Angeles
City County, County State of
California and known as the
"Mathews Vineyard" about ____
—situate in all Containing about
80 acres, more or less, bounded
North-Easterly from Street, Street
West by a Same Street that being
by Los Angeles garden., South East by
Juan St. and land and North East
by J R Mathews place —

Valued at $700.00

5. A lot of land situated in Los Angeles, Cal., Los Angeles County, State of California, bounded on the East by Main Street, on the North ... by ... Attorney recently purchased from the Estate of John Temple deed; on the West by New High Street, And on the North by lot of Philippe Colin —

together with the improvements on the said lot
Valued at $14,000.00

6. A lot situated in the Los Angeles City, Los Angeles County, State of California, bounded North by New High St., South by Andrea Almenares, ... East by N. Danston — same as the Chico Street; improvements — the improvements.
Valued at $600.00

7. A body of land situated in the ... County, State of California, known as "Azusa Rancho" containing the league of land... of land more or less — being the tract of land granted to A. Duarte by Juan B. Alvarado — bounded South by Public Lands

East by lands of Henry Dalton, by Public lands and West by Santa Anita Rancho —
Valued at $30,000.00

8. A body of land situated in ... Los Angeles County, State of California known as "Rancho Santa Anita" — bounded Northerly and ... West by land there belong to L. Roy; South by Public Land, and East by Azusa Rancho — containing 7000 acres more or less. Valued at $15,000.00

9. The equal undivided one half [½] interest in a quartz mining ... & Mines, in Azusa Ysabesta District, Kern County, California — Valued at $500.00

There are also lands in San Bernardino County, State of California — of which a schedule ... inventory will be made —

Total value of land making property $70,800.00

Personal property –

2347 Sheep, in Los Angeles County in
charge of Elijah Moulton who has them
under contract. Valued at $1 @ $1.50 .... 3,514.50
Horses) do. 3343 head @ $0.50
Mares) 20½ @ $10 per head 2,010
Colts)
Life this City
valued at $1

5 Stacks – 1 at 500. – 1 at 500. 200.
Norman Cattle in the charge
of Joseph L. Marie – with Ca.
                                              1/0
   Total 2114 head @ $7½
                                             ....
   valued at $ 1498

At the home place in Los Angeles City
the following property –

2 Mules 250
4 Horses .... @ 25. 100
2 Spring Wagons ...... .25. 50
1 Large Wagon .... " . 40
3 old setts of Harness .... " 10 30
1 " Spring Wagon Harness ..... 3.
1 Cutting Box 1
2 Saddles 10
1 Fan Mill 2
1 Gang Plow 125
1 Corn Sheller 2.50
   Net Value Personal Property – $ 8,366.00

— — —

Amount personal pro brought over — $8,366.00

5 Ropes of the Sheep Manager   2.50
1 Hy Max E.C. Rain   15.00
1 lot Harq. Iron   36.00
1 doz Picks   3.00
5 Se of the   3.75
1 Copper Weigh   @ 75
1 Wheel Barrow   3.00
4 Doz Chisels   2.00
24 Hoes   @ 1.50   6.00
Part of sett of Carpenter tool
                           @ 25   6.00
                            . 25   2.50
2 Truck Saws   5.00
3 Shovels   @ 50   1.00
5 Cultivan   @ 25   1.75
6 Axes   @ 1.00   5.00
1 Smith forge   @ 50   3.00
1 Cross Cut Saw   1.00
2 lott All No.   3.00
1 Jack   @ 25   .50
½ doz Pruning Knives   .50
1 Pruning Shears   @ 25   1.50
7 Pitch Fork   .50
2 Bone Boxes   @ 50   3.50
1 Riveting Hammer   .50   1.00
1 Nun saw   .50
2 Maze Nets   3.00
3 Plows   @ 5   1000
1 Corn Sheller   @ 5   3500
                           @ 5   1300
                                    2.00
                                $ 8,538.75

Mrs. Pro:

Mrs. Jno: prop:

$5,538.50

2 Wooden Racks	@25	.50
1 pair scales		16.00
2 Piano's	@ 20	
	@50	250.00
drawing Glasses		47.00
2 marbl. table	@10	20.00
3 Corner stands	3.	9.00
2 Clocks		33.00
1 sofa		15.00
1 large map		10.00
48 Chairs	@1	48.00
7 bed steads with Mattresses	@10	70.00
2 Wash stands	@15	30.00
1 Chest drawers		5.00
9 Bureaus	@10	30.00
1 desk		5.00
5 Wash stands	@1	5.00
2 Trunks	2	4.00
library & Table		50.00
7 Tables	@2	14.00
2 Cots		20.00
2 Closets	@2	4.00
1 cooking stove		5.00
3 Coffee Mills	@25	.75
6 brass Kettle	@3	18.00
1½ Sacks Coffee		30.00
9 Washing Tubs	50	1.50
1 hot air fan		5.00

Mrs. Jno: property $9,298.25

Mrs. Jno: property Brought over $9,298.25

1 Sewing Machine		1.00
2 Side Saddles	@5	5.00
54 Cans fruit	@5	2.50
1 lot preserves jars		1.50
1½ bbl Sugar		35.00
1 Medicine Chest		.50
1 lot Silver spoons		100.00
1 " dishes & c & c		10.00
1 family Chest		5.00
1 lot table fruit		
7 Connecting tubs	@10	70.00
2 Salt		300.00
1 Thrashing Press		5.00

Mrs. prop: $9,865.75

Notes

Emil Jaene	26.12, 1862			400.
Reuben Vaterman	rec 29/62 no int/100.			
W. A. Henson	Rec. (Aurora)	Rec 1/7/63	2½% Mo	
to D. Nilson	2000. Oct 25-2/63	2½% Mo		
to D. Nilson	1000. Nov. 1. 68	2% "		
C. S. Nilson	400. Feb 12/64	2% "		
Gest. Long	2000. since Sept	1¾% — no more since		
Carl Hann	2445.61 May 27.66	1½%		
to G. Nilson	1000.00 rec 11/62	2%		
N. Vahert	600.00 June 5/63	2%		
Henderson re and.	300. Apl 9/65	2%		
A. Henderson 1500, Minn 6/65 2% Jan Aug 1/65 11½%				

State of California }
County of Fresno } ss

Mathew Wolfskill, Joseph Wolfskill & Henry A Jurnis the _____ of the estate of William Wolfskill deceased, being duly sworn, says, that the annexed inventory contains a true statement of all the estate of the deceased that has come to the knowledge and possession of deponents and particularly of all money belonging to said deceased, and of all just claims of said deceased against _____

Joseph Wolfskill
Henry A Barrows
_____ Wolfskill

_____ of the Probate Court.
Deputy County Clerk and Deputy Clerk.

Estate of William Wolfskill deceased.

To B F Wilson & R F Teeple
    John Reel

To compensation for services in appraising said Estate—items as follows:
    _____ days service at $ 5 __ per day each. $15.00

Necessary disbursements—as follows:

the appraisers above named, being duly sworn, each for himself says, that the foregoing bill of items is correct and just, and that the services have been duly rendered as therein set forth.

B F Wilson.   R F Teeple
John Reel.

County of Fresno }

Subscribed and sworn to before me this 31st day of Oct 1866 A.D. 1866

B F Wilson
R F Teeple
John Reel

Joseph _____   Deputy County Clerk

San Marcos 700. Sum 13/63 Mo 14%
A Francis 550. May 23/63 " 1%
Carmen Reach 1000 Dec 10/63.
V Wolfskill 200 April 3/66 1 14%

1 Draft _____ Sac of Cal   1980.
  on Peronal Est._
April Cash in Bank of T S Lazard & Co   9052.17
       So loans Keeping to   10%   300.00
       Stephen A S Barrows   3922.66.
       " " John Turner   1983.08
       " Fox loan Mono Kings Co 16.Etc.   900.00

                                   $250.00
                            $ 114.136.44
                             $ 3.829.0 0
                            $ 117.965.44

We, the undersigned, duly appointed appraisers of the Estate of William Wolfskill did certify that the property mentioned in the foregoing appraisement has been duly exhibited to us, and we appraise the same at One hundred seventeen thousand nine hundred
* Sixty five & 44/100 dollars
Oct 31 1866

John Reel
R F Teeple
B F Wilson

IN THE MATTER OF THE ESTATE

OF

William Wolfskill,

DECEASED.

IN THE PROBATE COURT ———— COUNTY OF Los Angeles

County of ————

I, _Thomas A. Sanchez_ County Clerk of the ———— County of ————

and ex-Officio Clerk of the Probate Court thereof, do hereby certify that

Alden A. M. Jackson, Marcus Katz and _Jacob Elias_

have been duly appointed Appraisers of the Estate of _William Wolfskill_

deceased, by order of the Court, duly entered and recorded, on the 31th day of

October A. D. 186 6

WITNESS my hand and the seal of said Probate Court, this 31th day of October 186 6

J. D. Mott, CLERK,

By _Joseph Huber_ or _J. D._ DEPUTY CLERK.

State of California } ss.
County of San Bernardino }

Alden A. M. Jackson, Marcus Katz and Jacob Elias men

duly appointed Appraisers of the Estate of _William Wolfskill_ deceased,

being duly sworn, each for himself says, that he will truly, honestly and impartially appraise the property of

said estate which shall be exhibited to him according to the best of his knowledge and ability.

Alden A. M. Jackson
Marcus Katz
Jacob Elias

Subscribed and sworn to before me this 6th

———— day of Nov. A. D. 186 6,

A. F. Melrooms

J. Henry Miller Esq.

In the Matter of the
Estate of
Wm Wolfskill Dec'd

Appointment of
Appraisers in San Bernar
-dino County.

Filed November 27/66
J D Mott's Clerk
By Joseph Huber
Deputy

List of the Real Estate and Personal Property belonging to the estate of William Wolfskill deceased, situated in the County of San Bernardino, State of California —

viz:

Real property —

Lot No Two (2), Three (3), Four (4), Five (5), Fourteen (14), — Fifteen (15), Sixteen (16), Seventeen (17), & Eighteen (18) of 1 Block No. [] also Lot No. one (1), Two (2), Three (3) & Four (4) in Block No. Eleven (11) — all of the foregoing lots being of the five (5) acre Survey in the City & County of San Bernardino, State of California viz: known as the Trustee property situate upon place the foregoing — $4,500.00

also the mill privilege one half (½) No. Two (2), Three (3), Four (4), & Five (5), Six (6), Seven (7), Eight (8) & Nine (9), & Ten (10) of Block No. Eight (8) also of the same forty acres buildings, mill &c — $6,935.00

Property on which the mill is situated

also the mill privilege one half Lot No (39) Thirty Nine (39), Forty Three (43), Forty Three, (46) Forty Six (46), Forty Seven, No (52) fifty seven of the lots being the survey of the City and County of San Bernardino County State of California — all of which are lots among & according to the plan of survey of the Rancho of San Bernardino, filed of record in the office of the Recorder of said San Bernardino County — — $2,000.00

$8,935.00

Pasture lands —

(called the Greentree Mission Land of which 2 Leagues refered to in appendix to this Inventory

$7,692.00
$16,627.00

Personal property —

All other inventories, [?] Personal property

State of California }
County of Los Angeles }

We, [?] Mortgagor [?] Henry O. [?] and [?] and proper Mortgagor [?] the [?] of the estate [?] [?] of [?] deceased, being duly sworn, say that the foregoing [?] contains a true statement of all the estate of the deceased that has come to our knowledge [?] and which is situated in San Bernardino County, State of California, and [?] by of all money belonging to said deceased, and all just claims of said deceased [?] them [?] except the sum of [?] [?]

Subscribed and sworn to before me [?]

Mathias Wolfskill
N. [?] Barrows
Joseph Wolfskill

We, the undersigned, duly appointed appraisers for San Bernardino County, [?] of the State of [?] [?], do hereby certify that the foregoing inventory [?] in the foregoing appraisement [?] true [?] to my own [?] [?] [?] the same at [?]

[?] Jan [?] and [?] [?]

[?] Dudley
[?] [?]
[?] Dudley

San Bernardino County }
November 6th 1866 }

Estate of William Wolfskill dec'd
To [?] A M [?], [?] [?]
and army [?]
for [?] [?] in [?] as [?]
3 copies at [?] for [?] [?]
[?] [?] [?]
Received [?] [?]

[?] [?]
Nathan Katz

Bibliography

Bibliography

MANUSCRIPT COLLECTIONS

Bancroft Library, University of California, Berkeley.
  Archives of California. Departmental Records
  —— Departmental State Papers.
  Archivo de Gobernación. Mexico.
  Bancroft, Hubert H. Biographical Scraps.
  —— A Sketch of the Active Part Taken in the Historical Development of California by John R. Wolfskill, Sarchel Wolfskill and William Wolfskill.
  Botello, Narciso. Anales del sur de la California, 1833-47.
  Carson, Christopher. Kit Carson's Story as Told by Himself, n.d.
  Coronel, Antonio F. Documentos para la historia de California.
  Haraszthy, Arpad. Haraszthy Family Papers.
  Hayes, Benjamin. Notes on California Affairs.
  Kohler, Charles. Wine Production in California.
  Larkin, Thomas O. Accounts, 1840-1851.
  —— Documents for the History of California, 1839-1856.
  Marsh, John. Correspondence and Papers.
  Rowland, John. Lista de los que acompañan al sur, que suscribe en su llegado al territorio de la Alta California.
  Vallejo, Mariano G. Documentos para la historia de California, 1769-1850.
  Vega, Victoriano. Vida Californiana.
  Wilson, Benjamin D. Observations on Early Days in California.
  Wolfskill, John R. A Short Biographical Sketch.
  Yount, George. Chronicles of George C. Yount as dictated to Rev. Orange Clark.

CHURCH OF OUR LADY QUEEN OF THE ANGELS (OLD PLAZA), LOS ANGELES, CALIFORNIA. ARCHIVES.

Libro primero de Bautismos desde Marzo 6 de 1826 hasta Dic. 24 de 1848.

Libro tercero de Matrimonios Perteneciente a esta Misión de San Gabriel, Libro primero de Los Angeles.

CHURCH OF OUR LADY OF THE SORROWS, SANTA BARBARA, CALIFORNIA. ARCHIVES.

Lugo, María Magdalena. Birth Certificate; Baptismal Certificate.

HUNTINGTON LIBRARY, SAN MARINO, CALIFORNIA.

Mellus, Francis. Journal of Voyages to, from and along the Coast of California, 1838-1847.

Ritch, William G. Ritch Collection.

Stearns, Abel. Stearns Papers.

Wolfskill, Lewis. Correspondence and Papers.

Wolfskill, William. Ledger of Accounts, 1830-1832.

—— Ledger of Accounts, 1843-1854.

LOS ANGELES CITY ARCHIVES

Census of 1836; 1844.

Book of Deeds, vol. I.

Records of the *Ayuntamiento,* vols. I, II, IV, V, VI.

Translations, vols. I-IV.

LOS ANGELES COUNTY MUSEUM

Coronel, Antonio F. Coronel Collection.

Del Valle, Ignacio. Del Valle Collection.

LOS ANGELES PUBLIC LIBRARY

Burns, Annie Walker. Kentucky Vital Statistics. Ms 124.

NEW MEXICO, STATE ARCHIVES, SANTA FE

Mexican Archives of New Mexico, 1822-1831.

SPECIAL COLLECTIONS LIBRARY, UNIVERSITY OF CALIFORNIA, LOS ANGELES

Barrows, Alice Wolfskill. Correspondence and Papers.

Gillespie, Archibald Hamilton. Gillespie Papers.

Wolfskill, John. Deeds and Papers pertaining to Rancho San José de Buenos Ayres.

PRIVATE COLLECTIONS

Benton, Mrs. Charles E., of Los Angeles. Papers of Henry D. Barrows.

Cullen, Mrs. Thomas P., of Los Angeles. Diary and Papers of Henry D. Barrows.

—— Diary of Juana Wolfskill Barrows.

Dart, Mrs. Robert, of Sacramento, Calif. Papers of John R. Wolfskill.

Wolfskill, John C., of Los Angeles. Papers of William Wolfskill.

—— Wolfskill Genealogy, by Thomas W. Temple.

GOVERNMENT DOCUMENTS AND PUBLICATIONS

California State Agricultural Society, *Transactions*. Sacramento: State Printing Office, 1859.

California Superior Court Records. *Estate of William Wolfskill, Case no. 313.* Los Angeles County, California.

Hancock, Henry. *Report of the Surveyor General of California Made to the Secretary of the Interior on Land for the Year 1880.* Washington: Government Printing Office, 1881.

Hoffman, Ogden. *District Judge Reports of Land Cases Determined in the U.S. District Court for the Northern District of California, June term 1853 to June term 1858, incl.* San Francisco: Numa Herbert, 1862.

Jimeno, Manuel. *Index of Land Concessions from 1830-1845 and "Toma de Razón" or Registry of the Titles for 1844-45.* San Francisco: Lee and Carl, 1846.

Los Angeles County. *Book of Deeds.*

U.S. Census Office. *Census of the City and County of Los Angeles, California, for the Year 1850.* Reprint, Los Angeles, 1929.

—— Census 179 of Franklin County, *Pennsylvania Archives,* 5th Series, vol. 6, p. 119.

U.S. Congress. California and Mexico. 33 Cong., 2 sess., Ho. Doc. VI, no. 8. Washington, 1894.

—— Senate. Committee on Public Lands and Surveys. Mexican Land Grant Frauds, Hearings. 69 Cong., 2 sess., on Sen. Res. 333. Washington, 1927.

—— Senate. Report on the Subject of Land Titles in California, by William Carey Jones. 31 Cong., 1 sess., Sen. Doc. 18. Washington, 1892.

U.S. District Court Records. *The United States vs. George C. Yount,* Case no. 32. Records of the Northern District of California. San Francisco, 1854.

—— *The United States vs. William Wolfskill,* Case no. 232. Records of the Northern District of California. San Francisco, 1854.

U.S. Public Land Commission. Committee on Codification. *The Public Domain – Its History with Statistics.* Washington, 1880.

NEWSPAPERS

California Star. San Francisco, July 3, 1847-April 1, 1848.

Daily Alta California. San Francisco, Dec. 29, 1847; April 6, 1855; Oct. 12-14, 1866; Jan. 9, 1868.

Daily Evening Bulletin. San Francisco, Nov. 5, 1858; Dec. 17, 1858; Oct. 24-Nov. 8, 1859; Oct. 26, 1866.

Daily Examiner. Los Angeles, Aug. 21, 1888.

Daily Examiner. San Francisco, Jan. 19, 1869.

Los Angeles *Daily Commercial,* Oct. 26, 1880.

Los Angeles *Herald,* Oct. 15, 1873; Oct. 24-26, 1880.

Los Angeles *Semi-Weekly News,* May 1, 1866; Oct. 4-5, 1866.

Los Angeles *Star,* Feb. 14, 1852-Dec. 31, 1866; June 26, 1870; July 10, 1882.

Los Angeles *Tri-Weekly News,* Mar. 25, 1865; Sept. 19, 1865.

Los Angeles *World,* Jan. 1, 1886-Dec. 31, 1887.

Missouri Intelligencer. Franklin, Sept. 3, 1822; June 17, 1823; Aug. 5, 1825.

Niles National Register. Baltimore, Dec. 4, 1841.

Pico Weekly Chronicle. Los Angeles, Mar. 26, 1909.
Santa Ana *Herald,* June 20, 1886.
Southern Vineyard. Los Angeles, Mar. 20, 1858-Oct. 1, 1858.
Sunday Social World. Los Angeles, April 24, 1887.
Vacaville *Reporter,* June 5, 1897.
Vallejo *News-Chronicle,* Dec. 19, 1958.
Wilmington *Journal,* Jan. 1, 1857-Oct. 29, 1866.

BOOKS, ARTICLES, THESES

Armor, Samuel. *The History of Orange County, California.* Los Angeles: Historic Record Co., 1911.
Bakeless, John. *Daniel Boone.* New York: William Morrow & Co., 1939.
Baker, Charles C. "The Dispensing of Justice under the Mexican Regime," in *Annual Publications, Historical Society of Southern California,* x (1913), 36-40.
Bancroft, Hubert H. *History of California.* San Francisco: History Company, 1886-1890. 7 vols.
Barrows, Henry D. "John Wolfskill," in *Annual Report, Los Angeles County Pioneers of Southern California,* VIII (1913-14), 11-14.
—— "Los Angeles Fifty Years Ago," in *Annual Publications, Historical Society of Southern California,* VI (1905), 203-06.
—— "A Pioneer of Sacramento Valley," in *Annual Publications, Historical Society of Southern California,* IV (1897), 12-17.
—— "Pioneer Schools of Los Angeles," in *Annual Publications, Historical Society of Southern California,* VIII (1911), 62-66.
—— "Reminiscences of Los Angeles in the Fifties and Early Sixties," in *Annual Publications, Historical Society of Southern California,* III (1893), 55-62.
—— "The Story of a Native Californian 'Ramón Valenzuela'," in *Annual Publications, Historical Society of Southern California,* IV (1898), 114-18.
—— "Two Notable Pioneers – Col. J. J. Ayers and Geo. Hansen," in *Annual Publications, Historical Society of Southern California,* IV (1897).

Barrows, Henry D. "Water for Domestic Purposes vs. Water for Irrigation," in *Annual Report, Los Angeles County Pioneers of Southern California,* VII (1912-13), 64.

—— "William Wolfskill, the Pioneer," in *Annual Publications, Historical Society of Southern California,* V (1902), 290-97.

Bartlett, William C. "The Tropical Fruits of California," in *Overland Monthly,* I (September 1868), 263-68.

Baur, John E. "A President Visits Los Angeles: Rutherford B. Hayes' Tour of 1880," in *Historical Society of Southern California Quarterly,* XXXVII (March 1955), 33-47.

Beattie, George W. and Helen P. *Heritage of the Valley.* Pasadena: San Pasqual Press, 1939.

Becknell, Thomas. "The Journals of Capt. Thomas Becknell from Boone's Lick to Santa Fe and from Santa Cruz to Green River," in *Missouri Historical Review,* IV (January 1910), 65-84.

Bell, Horace. *Reminiscences of a Ranger or Early Times in Southern California.* Santa Barbara: Wallace Hebberd, 1927.

Bioletti, Frederic T. "A Short Sketch of the History of Wine Making in California," in *California Journal of Development,* XXIII (December 1933), 14-15, 45.

Boyd, Jessie Edna. Historical Import of the Orange Industry in Southern California. Unpublished M.A. thesis. University of California, 1922.

Broadhead, G.C. "Daniel Boone," in *Missouri Historical Review,* III (January 1909), 89-98.

Brown, Clara Spaulding. "La Ciudad de la Reina de Los Angeles," in *Overland Monthly,* n.s. I-II (June-July 1883), 579-88; 60-65.

Bryan, Will S. "Peculiarities of Life in Daniel Boone's Missouri Settlement," in *Missouri Historical Review,* IV (January 1910), 8-19.

Bryant, Edwin. *What I Saw in California.* New York: D. Appleton & Co., 1848.

Butterfield, H.M. "The Builders of California's Grape and Raisin Industry," in *The Blue Anchor*, xv (February 1938), 4-5.

California Winegrowers Association. "Vineyard Statistics," in *California Farmer*, i (January 2, 1863), 8-10.

Camp, Charles L., ed. "Chronicles of George C. Yount," in *California Historical Society Quarterly*, ii (April, 1923), 38-44.

Carosso, Vincent P. *The California Wine Industry, 1830-1895*. Berkeley: University of California Press, 1951.

Carr, Harry. *Los Angeles*. New York: D. Appleton-Century Co., 1935.

Carson, Christopher. *Kit Carson's Own Story of his Life as Dictated to Col. and Mrs. D. C. Peters*. Edited by Blanche C. Grant. Taos, New Mexico, 1926.

Cleland, Robert Glass. *Cattle on a Thousand Hills*. San Marino: Huntington Library, 1941.

—— *History of California: the American Period*. New York: Macmillan Co., 1923.

—— *The Irvine Ranch of Orange County*. San Marino: Huntington Library, 1962.

—— *This Reckless Breed of Men*. New York: Alfred A. Knopf, 1950.

Cline, Gloria Griffen. *Exploring the Great Basin*. Norman: University of Oklahoma Press, 1963.

Cloud, Roy W. *Education in California*. Stanford: Stanford University Press, 1952.

Coit, J. Eliot. *Citrus Fruits — An Account of the Citrus Fruit Industry with Special Reference to California Requirements and Practices and Similar Conditions*. New York: Macmillan Co., 1915.

Colburn, Frona E. *Wines and Vines of California*. San Francisco: Bancroft Company, 1889.

Cooper, Stephen. *Sketches from the Life of Major Stephen Cooper*. Oakland: Thompson & West, 1888.

Cronise, Titus Fey. *Natural Wealth of California.* San Francisco: H. H. Bancroft & Company, 1868.

Crystal, Helen Dormody. The Beginnings of Vacaville, California. Unpublished M.A. thesis. University of California, 1923.

Day, F.H. "Sketches of the Early Settlers of California: George C. Yount," in *Hesperian,* II (March 1859), 1-6.

—— "Sketches of the Early Settlers of California: Ziba Branch," in *Hesperian,* II (Oct. 1859), 337-39.

Downey, John G. "More About Orange Culture," in *Overland Monthly,* XII (June 1874), 560-62.

Duffus, R.L. *The Santa Fe Trail.* New York: Longmans, Green & Co., 1930.

Dunlap, Boutwell. "The Family of George C. Yount," in *California Historical Society Quarterly,* II (April 1923), 67-8.

Elliot, T.C. "Peter Skene Ogden, Fur Trader," in *Oregon Historical Society Quarterly,* XI (September 1910), 229-78.

Engelhardt, Zephyrin. *San Gabriel Mission and the Beginnings of Los Angeles.* San Gabriel: Mission San Gabriel, 1927.

Evans, Taliesin. "Orange Culture in California," in *Overland Monthly,* XII (March 1874), 235-244.

Ferril, Will C. "Missouri Military in the War of 1812," in *Missouri Historical Review,* IV (October 1909), 38-41.

Fish, A.C. "The Profits of Orange Culture," in *Golden Era,* XXXIX (March 1890), 114-122.

Goodwin, Cardinal. "John H. Fonda's Explorations in the Southwest," in *Southwestern Historical Quarterly,* XXIII (July 1919), 39-46.

Grant, Blanche C. *When Old Trails Were New – The Story of Taos.* New York: Press of the Pioneers, 1934.

Gregg, Josiah. *Commerce of the Prairies.* Edited by Max L. Moorehead. Norman: University of Oklahoma Press, 1954.

Gregory, Thomas J. *History of Solano and Napa Counties, California.* Los Angeles: Historic Record Company, 1912.

Guinn, James M. *Historical and Biographical Record of Los Angeles and Vicinity.* Chicago: Chapman Publishing Co., 1901.

—— *History of California and an Extended History of Los Angeles and Environs.* Los Angeles: Historic Record Co., 1915.

—— *History of California and an Extended History of its Southern Coast Counties.* Los Angeles: Historic Record Co., 1907.

—— "The Old Time Schools and Schoolmasters of Los Angeles," in *Annual Publications, Historical Society of Southern California,* III (1897), 7-15.

Hafen, LeRoy R. and Ann W. *The Old Spanish Trail.* Far West and Rockies Series, volume I. Glendale: Arthur H. Clark Co., 1954.

Hafen, LeRoy R. and Carl C. Rister. *Western America.* New York: Prentice-Hall, Inc., 1954.

Hancock, Ralph. *Fabulous Boulevard.* New York: Funk & Wagnalls Co., 1949.

Haraszthy, Agoston. *Grape Culture, Wines and Wine Making.* New York: Harper & Brothers, 1862.

Haraszthy, Arpad. "Wine Making in California," in *Overland Monthly,* VII (December 1871), 489-497.

Hargis, Donald E. "Native Californians in the Constitutional Convention of 1849," in *Historical Society of Southern California Quarterly* XXXVI (March 1954), 3-13.

Hayes, Benjamin. *Pioneer Notes from the Diaries of Judge Benjamin Hayes.* Los Angeles: private printing, 1929.

Hewitt, Randall H. "Orange Packing and Shipping," in *Annual Report, Los Angeles County Pioneers of Southern California,* VII (1912-13), 67-69.

Hill, Joseph J. "Ewing Young in the Fur Trade of the Far Southwest, 1822-1834," in *Oregon Historical Society Quarterly,* XXIV (March 1923), 1-35.

—— *The History of Warner's Ranch and its Environs.* Los Angeles: Young and McCallister, 1927.

—— "New Light on Pattie and the Southwestern Fur Trade," in *Southwestern Historical Quarterly,* XXVI (April 1923), 243-54.

—— "The Old Spanish Trail," in *Hispanic American Historical Review,* IV (August 1921), 444-73.

Hill, Joseph J. "Spanish and Mexican Explorations and Trade Northwest from New Mexico into the Great Basin," in *Utah Historical Quarterly,* III (January 1934), 3-23.

History of Howard and Cooper Counties, Missouri. St. Louis: National Historical Co., 1883.

Hittell, John S. "Notes on California Pioneers," in *Hutchings California Magazine,* V (November 1860), 209-11.

—— *The Resources of California.* San Francisco: A. Roman & Co., 1863.

—— "Wines of California," in *Pacific Monthly,* X (September 1863), 196.

Hodge, Frederick Webb. "Pioneers and Prices," in *Historical Society of Southern California Quarterly,* XXVIII (September 1946), 99-101.

Hulbert, Archer B. *Southwest on the Turquoise Trail.* Colorado Springs: Stewart Commission of Colorado College, 1933.

Hussey, John A. "Wolfskill Expedition to California, 1830-31," in *Grizzly Bear,* LVIII (February 1936), 18-20.

—— The Wolfskill Party in California. Unpublished M.A. thesis. University of California, 1923.

Hutchison, Claude B., ed. *California Agriculture.* Berkeley and Los Angeles: University of California Press, 1946.

Hyatt, T. Hart. *Handbook of Grape Culture.* San Francisco: H. H. Bancroft and Co., 1867.

Illustrated History of Los Angeles County, California. Chicago: Lewis Publishing Co., 1889.

Inman, Henry. *The Old Santa Fe Trail.* New York: Macmillan Co., 1897.

Jones, Idwal. *Vines in the Sun: A Journey through the California Vineyards.* New York: William Morrow & Co., 1949.

Jones, William Carey. *Land Titles in California.* Washington: Gideon & Co., 1850.

Lavender, David. *Bent's Fort.* New York: Doubleday & Co., 1954.

Lawrence, Eleanor F. "Mexican Trade between Santa Fe and Los Angeles, 1830-1848," in *California Historical Society Quarterly,* X (March 1931), 27-39.

—— The Old Spanish Trail from Santa Fe to California. Unpublished M.A. thesis. University of California, 1939.

Layne, J. Gregg. *Annals of Los Angeles.* San Francisco: California Historical Society, 1935.

—— "The First Census of the Los Angeles District," in *Historical Society of Southern California Quarterly,* XVIII (June 1936), 81-99.

Lelong, Byron Martin. *A Treatise on Citrus Culture in California.* Sacramento: State Printer, 1888.

Lorenz, A.J. *Centennial of the California Lemon.* Los Angeles: Sunkist Growers Assn., 1949.

Lugo, José del Carmen. "Vida de un Ranchero," trans. by Helen Pruitt Beattie, in *San Bernardino County Museum Association Quarterly,* VIII (Winter 1961).

Marshall, Thomas Maitland. "St. Vrain's Expedition to the Gila in 1826," in *Southwestern Historical Quarterly,* XIX (January 1916), 251-60.

McGroarty, John Steven. *California of the South.* Chicago: S. J. Clarke Publishing Co., 1935. 5 vols.

Morrison, Lorrin L. *Warner: The Man and the Ranch.* Los Angeles: Lorrin L. Morrison, 1962.

Morrow, William H. *Spanish and Mexican Private Land Grants.* San Francisco: Bancroft-Whitney Co., 1923.

Newhall, Ruth Waldo. *The Newhall Ranch.* San Marino: Huntington Library, 1958.

Newmark, Harris. *Sixty Years in Southern California.* Boston: Houghton Mifflin Co., 1930.

Oldham, Charles F. "Paper on California Wines," in *Society of Arts Journal* (London), XLII, pp. 195-201.

Pleasants, Joseph E. "A Fourth of July at San Fernando in 1856," in *Touring Topics,* XXII (February 1930), 49, 52-53.

Pleasants, Joseph E. "Los Angeles in 1856," in *Touring Topics,* XXII (January 1930), 36-37, 56.

—— "Ranging on the Mojave River in 1864," in *Touring Topics,* XXII (March 1930), 42-43.

Rixford, E. H. *The Wine Press and the Cellar.* San Francisco: Payot, Upham & Co., 1883.

Robinson, Alfred. *Life in California.* San Francisco: W. Doxie, 1891.

Robinson, W.W. *Los Angeles from the Days of the Pueblo.* San Francisco: California Historical Society, 1959.

—— *Ranchos Become Cities.* Pasadena: San Pasqual Press, 1939.

Ruxton, George F. *Ruxton of the Rockies.* Edited by LeRoy R. Hafen. Norman: University of Oklahoma Press, 1950.

Sabin, Edwin L. *Kit Carson Days, 1809-1868.* New York: Press of the Pioneers, 1935.

Salvator, Ludwig Louis. "A Flower from the Golden Land," in *Touring Topics,* XXI (January 1929), 14-19, 48.

Sanchez, Nellie Van de Grift. *California and Californians,* volume III. Chicago: Lewis Publishing Co., 1926.

Silver, J.S. "The Vineyards of California," in *Overland Monthly,* I (October 1868), 307-13.

"Some Historic Lines in Missouri," in *Missouri Historical Review,* III (July 1909), 253.

Spaulding, William A. "Early Chapters in the History of California Citrus Culture," in *California Citrograph,* VII (Jan.-March 1922), 66, 94-5, 122-24, 150-51, 169.

—— *History and Reminiscences of Los Angeles City and County, California.* Los Angeles: J. R. Finnell & Sons Publishing Co., n.d.

Stephenson, Terry E. *In the Shadows of Old Saddleback.* Santa Ana: High School Press, 1931.

Twitchell, Ralph Emerson. *Old Santa Fe,* volume I. Santa Fe: Old Santa Fe Press, 1913.

Von Blon, John L. "Here Oranges like Ruddy Lanterns Shine," in *Touring Topics,* XXV (November 1933), 12-14.

Wagner, Philip M. *A Wine-Grower's Guide.* New York: Alfred A. Knopf, 1945.

Warner, J.J., Judge Benjamin Hayes and Dr. J. P. Widney. *An Historical Sketch of Los Angeles County, California.* Los Angeles: Louis Lewin & Co., 1876.

Warner, J.J. "Reminiscences of Early California – 1831 to 1846," in *Annual Publications, Historical Society of Southern California,* VII (1908), 176-193.

Whitwell, Gertrude Howard. "William Davis Merry Howard," in *California Historical Society Quarterly,* XXVII (June 1948), 105-112.

Willard, Charles Dwight. *History of Los Angeles City.* Los Angeles: Kingsley-Barnes & Neuner Co., 1901.

Wilson, Iris H. "Early Southern California Viniculture," in *Historical Society of Southern California Quarterly,* XXXIX (September 1957), 242-49.

—— William Wolfskill and the Development of Southern California. Unpublished M.A. thesis. University of Southern California, 1957.

Wilson, J. Albert. *History of Los Angeles County.* Oakland: Thompson & West, 1880.

Wine Advisory Board. *Wine Handbook Series.* San Francisco: California Wine Advisory Board, 1943.

"Wine Making in California," in *Overland Monthly,* VII (December, 1871)

Wine of California. Atchison, Topeka and Santa Fe Railway Co., 1937.

Wood, Ellen Lamont. "Samuel Green McMahan," in *California Historical Society Quarterly,* XXIII (December 1944), 289-300.

Woodbury, A.M. "The Route of Jedediah Smith in 1826," in *Utah Historical Society Quarterly,* IV (April 1931), 35-46.

Workman, Boyle. *The City that Grew.* Los Angeles: Southland Publishing Co., 1936.

Index

Index